THE ARTS
WITHOUT
MYSTERY

THE ARTS
WITHOUT
MYSTERY

DENIS DONOGHUE

THE BRITISH BROADCASTING CORPORATION

Acknowledgements are made to Faber and Faber for the use of extracts from *The Waste Land*, 'Little Gidding' from *The Four Quartets*, and 'Whispers of Immortality' by T.S. Eliot, all taken from *Collected Poems 1909–1962*, and from 'Of Mere Being' by Wallace Stevens, taken from *Opus Posthumous*, and to Chatto and Windus for the use of extracts from 'Your Teeth are Ivory Towers' from *Collected Poems* by William Empson. The essay 'On the Limits of a Language', reprinted here, first appeared in *The Sewanee Review*, vol 85, no 3, 1977.

Published by the British Broadcasting Corporation
35 Marylebone High Street, London W1M 4AA

ISBN 0 563 20182 7 (hardback)
ISBN 0 563 20248 3 (paperback)

First published 1983
© Denis Donoghue 1983

Set in 11/12pt Monophoto Van Dijck and printed
in England by Jolly & Barber Ltd, Rugby

CONTENTS

To Frances

INTRODUCTION

The invitation was tentative. Not: would I like to give the Reith Lectures for 1982? But: if the Governors of the BBC were to invite me to give the Reith Lectures for 1982, would I be able to offer a theme suitable to the occasion? I assumed I was not expected to propose a topic in any of the areas surveyed by recent Reith lecturers; the disposition of nuclear weapons, the qualifications of doctors for certain life-or-death decisions they take, the character of the Christian Church in a world supposedly governed by political considerations. If I were to propose six lectures on the later poetry of T.S. Eliot or Wallace Stevens, the offer would certainly be regarded as a joke or a vivacity; not to be thought of. It soon emerged that a fairly general topic in 'the Arts' would be received with interest.

My first notion was to say something about modern literary criticism or, making a leap into broader contexts, to consider what has been going on, more generally, in the criticism of the arts. But that notion didn't survive. I don't know what's going on in the specialist journals concerned with opera, architecture, rock music, or whatever. The possibility of reducing my ignorance in those matters didn't strike me as plausible. Gradually, I found myself offering to say something about the arts as a constituent of modern societies; or rather, as a factor in public life. The lectures wouldn't be about the arts, or about any one of them, but about the way or ways in which they enter upon public life. Are they received on the assumption that they are events like any other, or unlike any other? Or are they thought to be things or events 'with a difference'?

I didn't want to talk about the subject in an apocalyptic style, or to represent the arts in a relentless association with what Robert Frost called 'the larger excruciations'. Such a style, even if I could rise to it·or fall upon it, would make me sound like a spiritual terrorist. At the same time, I was convinced that the ways in which the arts are received in modern society are mostly unsatisfactory. A work of art is in some sense mysterious; but I see no evidence, in contemporary criticism, that the mystery is acknowledged or respected. Two reasons suggest themselves: one, that knowledge, the dominant force in our engagement with experience, cannot admit mystery or respect it; and two, that discursive practices don't recognise what can't be explained. While I was working on the Reith Lectures, two passages, one from St Augustine, the other from E.M. Cioran, kept coming into my mind. From Augustine: 'Whatever is understood by knowledge is limited by the understanding of the knowledge: even what can be called ineffable is not ineffable.' From Cioran: 'The indigence of language renders the universe intelligible.'

Now a note for American readers. The Reith Lectures are given once a year on BBC (radio), usually in November and December. Six lectures, they go out on Wednesdays on Radio 4, are repeated on Sundays on Radio 3, and are published week by week in the BBC's magazine *The Listener*. Some Reith Lectures, including mine, are transmitted again on the BBC World Service. The Radio 4 audience is deemed to consist of a fairly general and reasonably well-informed body of listeners. Radio 3 listeners are assumed to be more specifically interested in the theme: they listen mostly to classical music, and are addressed in a rather unhurried style. I had no fault to find with those conditions.

So I set about writing the lectures. Several drafts were required: it was hard to get the tone right, I was alluding to too many works of art which the audience would not necessarily have read, heard, or seen. Besides, as soon as you mention 'mystery', aren't you talking about religion while pretending not to? How to distinguish between mystery, enigma, problem, crux, and other forms of opacity? If I tried to make the necessary distinctions, would I still have an audience when I had made them? Then there was the hardest question: can anything useful be said about a theme as diverse as the reception of the arts, which – given a sufficiently liberal definition – would include Henry James's novels, the Boomtown Rats on TV, Bette Midler in *Divine Madness*, John Ashbery's 'Self- Portrait in a Convex Mirror', Edvard Munch's paintings, Stanley Drucker and the New York Philharmonic Orchestra playing Nielsen's Clarinet Concerto, the AT&T Building in New York, John Lewis playing 'Django', Godard's *Le Petit Soldat*, the New York City Ballet in Balanchine's *Robert Schumann's Davidsbündlertänze*, the Piazzetta exhibition in Venice, Stieglitz's photograph of Georgia O'Keeffe, Jonathan Miller's production of *Rigoletto*? 'And this, and so much more.'

In the event, my addiction to the spoken word survived the constraints attendant upon preparing six half-hours of it. But another sentence from Augustine occurs to me: 'I have done nothing but wish to speak; if I have spoken, I have not said what I wished to say.' I am glad to have this opportunity of including, sometimes in a note, something I wanted to say but didn't have time or the right context for saying. I have printed, as Part I of each chapter, the lectures as I gave them. The shoulder notes are my later interjections. The commentaries include further things, developments of the argument, which I have had to hold over till now. The printed page has certain advantages over the spoken word, though I don't enjoy making that concession.

D.D.

ONE

THE ZEALOTS OF EXPLANATION

The painter Jasper Johns once remarked: 'I can imagine a society without any art at all, and it is not a bad society'.* I wonder what he meant; that the ways of art are intolerably oblique, and that for much of the time we want to live directly, we want to act as if immediacy were possible, in violence, revolution, or anarchy? Or that art gets in the way of other things, perhaps higher causes? It's entirely possible not only to relegate art to a secondary position but to think that art may be a nuisance. Johns may not have had anything very specific in mind: he may just have been appalled, for the moment, by the difficulty of art, or by the arbitrariness of the whole activity. He may have meant that it would be splendid if art weren't a separate thing, to be cultivated by those who are interested in it.

To composer-philosopher-sage John Cage.

Wouldn't it be better if the artistic impulse were fulfilled rather than humiliated in the ordinary run of daily life; if our social arrangements were to take into account not only justice but beauty? The philosopher John Dewey once imagined a time when 'the collective life that was manifested in war, worship and the forum knew no division between what was characteristic of these places and operations, and the arts that brought colour, grace, and dignity into them'. According to such a vision, the arts§ didn't exist as separate interests, the spoils of power, money, and leisure, but as enhancements, indistinguishable from the ordinary life they adorned. But I hope Johns meant something different – that he would prefer art not to exist at all than that it should exist as a commodity among commodities, its mystery removed. I want to talk about the arts in relation to the mystery that surrounds them, not as a problem to be cleared up but as the very condition in which they appear at all. In that sense mystery is to be acknowledged, not resolved or dispelled.

§ 'He hasn't defined what kind of art he's talking about: is it the punk poet, as well as Henry James?' It is: discriminations between the punk poet and H.J. can be made at any time.

It has become a scandal to speak of mystery. Many people regard talk of it as sheer mystification, a pretentious claim upon profundity as if the only situation worth talking about defeated every reasonable attempt to deal with it. But I want to reinstate mystery and to distinguish it from mere bewilderment or mystification. One of the strongest motives in modern life is to explain everything and preferably to explain it away. The typical mark of modern critics is that they are zealots of explanation, they want to deny to the arts their mystery, and to degrade mystery into a succession of problems.* But the effort is perverse.

See Appendix, page 21.

The philosopher Gabriel Marcel has distinguished a mystery from a problem in this way. 'A problem', he says 'is something met with which bars my passage. It is before me in its entirety. A mystery, on the other hand, is something in which I find myself caught up, and whose essence is therefore not to be before me in its entirety. . . . It is a proper character of problems to be reduced to detail: mystery, on the other hand, is something which cannot be reduced to detail.' When we refer, for instance, to the mystery of Being, we don't mean that it is something that comes to our attention as an obscurity, so that we can regard the obscurity as the first stage of clarification – as if at a later stage the issue would become clear or at worst clearer. If Being is a mystery, it is a mystery through and through, not a difficulty to be cleared up.

If we want to take the mystery out of life, it's because mystery is thought of as an insult to our intelligence; that the part we play in it is merely one of bewilderment. A character in Yeats's play *The Resurrection* says: 'What if there is always something that lies outside knowledge, outside order? What if the irrational return?' The gist of the matter is: a problem is something to be solved,§ a mystery is something to be witnessed and attested. By admitting this distinction I don't have to take a vow of silence and confess that on the arts there is nothing to be said. There is much to be said, short of an explanation. I'm not required to drive discussion of the arts into gorgeous or demonic nonsense.

§*C.S.Peirce's concept of 'the Dynamoid Object' is, for me, a problem. I have tried and failed to understand it. I am ready to believe that others with a different intellectual training can understand it. Similarly with the details we call conundrums, enigmas, a crux in logic, a still un-explained issue in astrophysics.*

The removal of mystery from the arts is one of the ways in which our society tries to tame the occult and its offence. In all the stories which have been inter-preted as bearing upon the presence of the artist in the world, there is a recurring pattern, a motif of strangeness. Prometheus stole fire from the gods and gave it to man, knowing that man needed it for some phase of his development and that the gods would not want to see him developed in that way. In another story the god Heracles gave Philoctetes a bow which was uncannily accurate, it never failed to hit the mark. One day Philoctetes was bitten by a snake. The wound suppurated, and it became so loathsome in its smell that Philoctetes's companions removed him to the island of Lemnos and sailed off to Troy without him. He remained banished for ten years; the wound hadn't healed. But it was revealed to the Greeks that they would never defeat the Trojans without Philoctetes and his bow. So they brought him back, he defeated Paris in single combat, and Troy was taken.

The story tells of the artist in a world which is alien to him.* His gift is uncanny and perhaps for that reason it seems loathsome till it is needed: it tells a truth people don't want to hear. In the story, the people realise at last that they need this truth, and they are ready to put up with the foul smell to have it. There, I suppose, the allegory breaks down for us. Modern society doesn't look to art for its salvation, or

> *'He referred to all artists and critics as males.' In what follows, the reader is invited to pronounce 'him' and 'his' as 'her' if he or she wishes to do so.

even for its wisdom. A poem, a novel, or a painting is never what a society thinks it needs. Indeed the relation between a society and the arts is never one of need, though it is sometimes one of enhancement or national pride. It's only in retrospect that a work of art may be seen to have defined the society that provoked it. Sometimes it's the only remaining evidence that the society it emerged from even existed, and the only justification for anyone's continuing interest in it. All of these stories speak of need and compulsion, of going beyond the limit. The artistic vision is in some way ineffable, unspeakable, it deflects every attempt to pin it down by knowledge or to define it in speech. The stories say that art is not to be assimilated to the comfortable ways of a society. The artist is an eagle, not a dove.§

> §In the story of Orpheus, the musician-poet is torn to pieces by the Thracian women: his head and lyre are thrown into the river, but the song persists.

In the Preface to *The Tragic Muse* Henry James said that the relation between art and society is one of conflict, and that the conflict is 'one of the half-dozen great primary motives', presumably because it touches upon many other motives once you let it spread. It's surprising, at first glance, that James thought it such a great theme; it could be regarded, on a damp morning, as a minor problem, a bother to a mere handful of people. But it's easy to think of the artist as representing not only his colleagues in the arts but anyone who feels, on good evidence or bad, that he is homeless in the world in which he lives. There's a passage in Italo Svevo's *Confessions of Zeno* where Zeno asserts that 'it is perfectly possible for someone to be conscious of possessing a very lofty intellect, even though that consciousness is the only proof he has of it.' It's equally possible for someone to be conscious of possessing an acute artistic gift on the same meagre evidence: the sentiment, given life by the desire for it, is all one needs. So James's theme speaks to anyone who feels his talents for whatever reason unemployed, and who believes them to be extraordinary. He didn't say whether the conflict between art and society is good or bad for art. My own understanding is that we receive the arts most completely not when we pay lip service to them but when the relation between art and society is mostly one of conflict and suspicion, if not one of hostility.

In *The Tragic Muse* James presents the conflict as one between art and politics, or rather between the diverse claims exerted by each. As a nuance, he assigns both motives to one character, Nick Dormer. There is a scene in which Nick wanders through the National Gallery in London, looking at paintings by Titian, Rubens, Gainsborough, and Rembrandt. His interests are divided between a desire to become a painter and a desire, which he understands as a duty, to go into politics. When his mind recoils from politics, it is because he thinks the vocation crude, it doesn't allow for shades and niceties of feeling. When it recoils from art, it's because art seems useless. When he talks about art, he sounds rather like Jasper Johns. 'These great works of art,' he thinks, are 'a poor business, only well enough in their small way.' Their place was inferior and 'their connection with the life of man casual and slight'. The worst you could say about politics at least was that it was 'a clumsy system for applying and propagating the idea'; the idea Nick has in mind is progress, the advancement of social and public life.

But why should there be antagonism between politics and art?* Isn't there room for both? The trouble is that both politics and art are universalist in their ambition, each claims a total vision of life. More emphatically, artists have resented the claim that politics knows what reality is, and that this knowledge is fully represented in political institutions. Of course there is

*'He spoke of an antagonism between the arts and politics as if "the arts" were something apart from politics, merely an aesthetic and not also a social practice.' Not so:

more than one way to engage with society. Like Dickens and Arnold, you can move freely, sometimes charming society, sometimes shaming it out of its complacency. Or, like Henry James, you could enjoy its social amenity while keeping your soul and your art intact, analysing the obscure relations of personal and social manners.§ More generally, the artist could take up an ironic or subversive attitude toward social convention. A motto for this gesture is Kenneth Burke's: 'When in Rome, do as the Greeks.'

But on the whole, serious artists in the past hundred years or so have assumed that it is morally disreputable for them to identify their values with those of middle-class society. There is in fact much to be said for bourgeois society even when we insist on degrading it by calling it bourgeois, but artists have rarely wanted to say any of it. One of the aims of modern art and literature has been to escape from the middle class and what Ezra Pound called its 'accelerated grimace'.

the arts are the most available image of an alternative life, an adversary image if the official life is understood as enforced social practice. (But this question arises later, in response to an objection from Terry Eagleton, page 27.)

§ *Or, like Emily Brontë, articulate passions that refuse to be domesticated: like Rimbaud, make repudiation a way of life, even unto silence and death. Sartre: 'The writer gives society a guilty conscience.'*

So the arts have appealed to pleasure rather than duty, interrogation rather than conformity; they thrive upon suspicion rather than consensus, the creative speech of poetry rather than the stereotypes of daily life. We would be surprised to read a good poem about urban clearance or the EEC. The artist tries to make a space for himself, if necessary a 'world elsewhere', rather than submit to the anonymity, the crowdedness, a mass-society would force upon him. In avant-garde art, these gestures of dissociation have sometimes been maintained to the point at which many people can see nothing in them but spiritual terrorism, like the fractured face in a Picasso portrait. In extreme cases, the gesture amounts to a rage for the absolute, as if nothing could satisfy, so long as it remains finite. So we have the demonic aspect of art, which is sometimes true mystery and sometimes its false face, mere mystification.

The nineteenth-century artist kept his soul, as far as possible, by withholding assent to official purposes. As the price to be paid for that spiritual privilege, his art emphasised difference rather than continuity of experience; a certain purity of form, only to be achieved by transcending the ordinary world. There is always a risk of weightlessness in his images or, in his voice, a suggestion of falsetto. He achieves form as a desperate choice, and we sense everything that has had to be kept out of the picture to make it become what it is. There is also the artist's particular form of vanity, the assumption that he is free of ideology, he is the exemplary manifestation of purity of heart. At an extreme point the artist feels the need to constitute art as a separate reality, with the implication that this is the true thing. Daily life is then represented as false, enforced by a society that finds lies more profitable than truth.

It has been common to see the artist as he has often seen himself, a man apart, doomed to bear his vision in an alien world. There are many ways of reaching this image. One of them is by holding a concept of the imagination as a special power or attribute. Some people have argued that imagination is much the same as perception, that the only difference is one of degree. But others maintain that imagination is the special capacity to posit something as not being real, and to take hold of such images in the composition of a work of art.

A man of imagination is not debarred from being also a man of perception, but if we regard the imagination as a distinctive power, creative and visionary, we set the artist apart and ascribe a peculiar destiny to him. He would not necessarily be better than other people: in the qualities which depend upon perception and memory, he might be worse. He might be ruthless, dishonest, immoral. He might exaggerate the scale of his gift, and think it justified incidental acts of turpitude. But in any case he would think of himself as different from other people. Dylan Thomas, John Berryman, Robert Lowell, Brendan Behan and Mark Rothko seem to have insisted on fulfilling the image of the doomed artist, as if their gift were a fatal wound. It's true that many people ruin themselves who are not artists; but people don't offer their not being artists as a reason for their having ruined themselves. The image of the doomed artist has retained its power because of the association of the artist with transgression, genius, the role of scapegoat, the sacrificial victim. We don't know what to make of this image. On the whole we try to include the artist in the forms of our knowledge, but if he rejects our embrace we know that in some profound sense he is right, he knows he is not really one of us. Art does not confirm the reality we normally think we know and possess. In fact, art is permanently antagonistic to our sense of reality because it makes a space for those images which our sense of reality excludes.

On the whole, critics of the arts aligned themselves with artists in repudiating the common middle-class world. Sometimes the critic saw himself as a mediator between an estranged artist and the common world from which he had withdrawn; often by showing that the artist's difficulty is not wanton or pretentious. Or the critic strengthened the artist's resolve, offering him the support of a sympathetic audience. Or he tried to place beside the work of art not a translation of its form but a set of meditations companionable to the work. The critic assumed that his true work was discrimination, the act of judgement and valuation. Criticism begins with the sensory experience of someone engaged with a work of art, but it is not complete until the analysis of sensation has been brought, in T.S. Eliot's phrase, 'to the point of principle and definition'. That phrase implies critical discrimination, because only in discrimination is the question of principle fully present and the question of definition adequately challenged. It's up to the reader to take the poem or the novel in that spirit.

When an art is changing, with new forms competing for space with older forms; when nothing like orthodoxy prevails; then the critic has to question his own relation to the art, and come to an understanding of it. He can't rely on an inherited relation. When F.R. Leavis wrote *New Bearings in English Poetry* in 1932, the major works in modern poetry were already there, but they were not in place, their mutual relations were not understood. Leavis's presentation of modern poetry essentially in terms of Hopkins, Eliot, and Pound was a work of critical discrimination.*

The problem now is that the relation between the arts and society has changed in ways which make many of these traditional critical enterprises redundant. There has been a change in the way artists see themselves, and the way in which society acknowledges them. The antagonism I mentioned between bourgeois and bohemian, duty and pleasure, constraint and freedom has been dissolved. Serious artists don't think of themselves as avant garde, on the subversive margin of society, driven there by capitalism and the corruption of the market. The division of society into middle-class liberals and the rest has lost its meaning. In the West it's only in theory, in university lecture-halls and ICA debates, that an alternative to liberalism is even mooted, and then it's mooted by people, of the Left and Right, who wouldn't think of giving up the satisfactions of middle-class life. In certain post-Marxist theories bourgeois liberalism is supposed to have ended, but in

*A rival critical enterprise would propose to understand modern poetry by representing Whitman or Hardy rather than Hopkins as the crucial inaugurative poet. In music, Constant Lambert's Music, Ho! (1934) made a strong case for regarding the history of modern music as exemplified mainly by Debussy, Stravinsky, Satie, Sibelius, and Schoenberg.

practice it survives. Indeed, it's impossible to point to a country in which a revolution of the Left or the Right has produced, in practice, social and personal values different from those of ordinary bourgeois societies. It's still possible to maintain a sense of divided interests within middle-class life; by accepting its mixture of satisfactions and irritations with reservations in one degree or another. We can devise 'techniques of trouble' to maintain a sense of scruple. Philosophers can undermine knowledge and regard it as mere self-delusion. But these troubles are largely self-induced, they are scruples arising from refinements of luxury, so they don't add up to anything more than a theoretical revolution, an apocalyptic seminar. Fortunately, they die of their own excess. Who talks any longer about 'the impossibility of communication', a problem we thought so incorrigible, a few years ago, that we mistook it for our fate?

Thirty or forty years ago it was commonly assumed that there were higher values than those administered by our official institutions; government, law, the market, the banks. It was supposed that religion, education, and the arts had a special concern for the higher values. The morality of the arts was to bring forward what the official institutions chose to forget; intimate subjective experience. The arts took up that experience and made it their main business. The poet John Crowe Ransom argued that the function of a genuine society is to instruct its members how to transform the values of instinct and appetite into aesthetic values; and he associated aesthetic values with those of religious conviction. He thought that societies might be persuaded to rise above their ordinary selves by observing the rituals of religion and art. In a different account R.P. Blackmur said that the purpose of literature, as of all intellect creative or critical, is to remind the powers that be, simple and corrupt as they are, of the forces they have to control. Ransom reminded our institutions of what is beyond their offices, though still within the reach of a leap of spirit. Blackmur reminded them of what is beneath them, unacknowledged, the old mole in the cellar. But in both these versions, the arts are assumed to be privileged; they know more by way of rituals and traditions than anyone knows in his mere individuality.

It's rare, these days, to hear the arts proclaimed in this way. No one dares to hope that middle-class society would be transformed, persuaded beyond its ordinary character by observing the rituals of art. It's still possible to find critics who want to shame middle-class society out of its conventions and undermine its power; mostly by presenting as sinister the same values which society presents elsewhere as laws of nature. But the writings of these critics move with significant speed into purely theoretical issues. Only when there is real belligerence between official and unofficial values is a worthwhile art possible; and middle-class society has discovered how to achieve its victory by pretending that nobody has been defeated. Especially since the turmoil of 1968, societies have learnt that they can deal with dissent by incorporating it. Orthodoxy can be expanded to accommodate heresy, and when the fuss dies down, it can contract again to its norm. The soft answer turneth away wrath, especially if it is accompanied by grants, fellowships and other felicities. The universities discovered that they could take Modernism off the streets by offering courses on its favourite texts.

In their turn, artists have come to terms with industrial capitalism, and some of them are even willing to enjoy it. The art critic Harold Rosenberg has maintained that the change came with Pop Art, which demonstrated that art doesn't need esoteric images or sanctified motifs, it can deal happily enough with standard domestic objects. 'Since the advent of Pop Art', he says, 'no influential American art movement has been either overtly or tacitly hostile to the "majority culture". Today, both the alienation of the artist and the antagonism of public opinion to art have been successfully liquidated.'* In any case there has been a truce. I suspect that hostility has been replaced by indifference. People have to ignore so much, these days, of what they see and hear that the outrageous doings of an artist are easy to deal with.

> *Long before Pop Art, Gropius and his colleagues accepted without fuss the conditions provided by technology.

In 1877 John Ruskin disliked the Whistler 'Nocturne' he saw at the Grosvenor Gallery and referred to 'the Cockney impudence by which a coxcomb could ask two hundred guineas for flinging a pot of paint in the public's face'. I doubt if anyone today, even an art critic, would bother to lose his temper, or throw it away, no matter what paintings he saw. If you don't like a painting, you walk away. There is still a certain edginess in the public response to high-brow music: a little of it goes a long way in concert programmes, if a general audience is expected to attend. But on other fronts the war is over. You can hardly play an electric guitar and maintain an aesthetic objection to technology. Besides, artists have discovered that there are constructive possibilities in the new mechanisms: electronic music, tape, digital recordings, video, intermedia of many kinds.* The reception of the arts is now technological through and through; Zeffirelli's production of *La Bohème* on television, *Brideshead Revisited* as the book of the television series.

The end of the war has made a difficulty for critics: they no longer know what they are supposed to be doing. So long as the artist was in conflict with respectable society, the critic's job was clear. But now he finds that the artist has made a separate peace with society. There is no further need of a mediator or a supporter. So a few critics have taken up the avant-garde function on their own authority; they have declared themselves independent, and have moved into philosophy. But most critics have remained uncomfortably on the margin of the arts, spending their time not in criticism but in description.

But in fact there is much work to be done in a discriminating way, or in a diagnostic way, especially where the work of art seems to proclaim itself mysterious. At the end of Peter Shaffer's play *Amadeus*, for instance, the central character Salieri, who is about to cut his throat, addresses the audience. He tells them that they are, like himself, failures, mediocrities: 'I was born a pair of ears and nothing else. It is only through hearing music that I know God exists. Only through writing music that I could worship. All around me men seek liberty for Mankind. I sought only slavery for myself. To be owned – ordered – exhausted by an *Absolute*. This was denied me, and with it all meaning.'

Nothing in the play up to this point has justified a claim upon the Absolute. Salieri's motives, as they have been presented, are petty enough to be understood without recourse to divinity or divination. The scene is not mystery but mystification; it is spurious in the grandeur it claims, just as spurious as the thrill middle-class audiences are expected to feel when they are denounced as fellow mediocrities by a man with a razor in his hand, about to demonstrate that he is unmediocre enough to cut his throat. Shaffer is trying to give his Salieri a force of radiance which nothing shown in the play warrants. Mystification is his recourse to false altitude, which in a dim light looks like the real thing. The sublimity is specious, as specious as the comforting implication, throughout *Amadeus*, that art is the modern substitute for religion.

There isn't much point in having the arts at all unless we have them with all their interrogative power.§ They are not cosy or ornamental. Critics have

20

collaborated in making them seem cosy, assuring us that they won't hurt a bit. If the arts don't hurt, why have them? It's only modern vanity which supposes that everything can be known or that only what is knowable has a claim upon our interest. The artist and the priest know that there are mysteries beyond anything that can be done with words, sounds or forms. If we want to live without this sense of mystery, we can of course, but we should be very suspicious of the feeling that everything coheres and that the arts, like everything else, fit comfortably into our lives.

> *his understanding that 'great artists are not transcribers of the scheme of things; they are its rivals'. In sum: 'all art is a revolt against man's fate.' The orthodoxy of discourse is concerned to transcribe the scheme of things, starting with the unearned assertion that the object of its attention is indeed the scheme of things.*

Appendix Note

For instance? In the BBC2 *series* 100 Great Paintings, *the critic Richard Cork, introducing Kandinsky's 'Improvisation 6', suggested that the content of the painting is the account, in St Mark's Gospel, of Christ's Resurrection and the scene at the tomb. 'So it's hardly fanciful to suggest,' he said, 'that the huge red block held by the figure on the right, whose head is crowned by a burnished halo, might be the stone rolled away from Christ's tomb: and the figure on the left, clutching a long stretch of blue drapery, may equally well be the man in the "long white garment" who, Saint Mary claims, was inside the empty sepulchre.' Cork's 'may' and 'might' are decorously modest, his interpretation can't be disproved. But it diminishes the painting. Not that another interpretation of the 'strong narrative content' would be any better. It is pointless to try to be more specific than the painting itself, from which Kandinsky eliminated anything that would individualise the two 'figures'. The more we look at the painting, the less pronounced its 'narrative content' becomes; and the stronger our sense that the energy of the work is entirely internal. The figures are like those that children draw, in one respect: no attempt is made to circumvent the fact that the surface, paper or canvas, is limited to two dimensions. They are figures all boundary and no mass; they have no substance or volume but, replete with indefinite relation, claim just so much privilege as accompanies that character. No psychology attends them. The more we look at the painting in this spirit, the more we find the differentiation of the figures from the other shapes that inhabit the canvas receding. What we find ourselves feeling is not that we want another interpretation than Cork's but that the painting testifies to whatever in the world refuses to be reduced to a narrative content or a psychological characterisation.*

Commentary

The Reith Lectures were discussed in *Voices*, a TV programme broadcast by ITV on Channel Four (London) on 26 January 1983. The participants were Robert Hutchison, Peter Maxwell Davies, Melvyn Bragg, Terry Eagleton and myself. The programme established very little, except that those of us who engage in communication by one means or another are naive if we think that communication, in any real sense, is ever achieved. The discussion lasted seventy-five minutes, with two commercial breaks. My colleagues, who were supposed to oppose and challenge my argument, mainly gave evidence that they had misunderstood it. Melvyn Bragg, a TV personality, was brittle and defensive about the personalising habit of arts programmes on television. Peter Maxwell Davies was grateful to TV for making him better-known than he would otherwise be, though he agreed that this argument was beside my point. Robert Hutchison moderated the discussion. Terry Eagleton's position was predictably consistent with the version of Marxism he has offered in several books.

It was Eagleton who raised, and kept coming back to, the political question; mostly in two assertions. The first was that my work belongs to 'the great tradition of gloom in cultural commentary'; he mentioned Coleridge, Arnold, and Leavis as precursors in this tradition. The gloom is supposed to issue from the critic's feeling that virtually everything in contemporary life is valueless, that nothing worthwhile is to be sought in politics or by way of political change. Value is to be found only in certain works of art, which must therefore be protected against vulgar tampering. Eagleton's second assertion was 'that mystery is an authoritarian concept to use about the arts', and that I am really saying 'there are certain truths, certain meanings intuitively available to certain people; either you see it or you don't.' Elitism, in short.

Eagleton's argument, though he didn't quite succeed in making it, became clear enough: he accused me of driving a wedge between politics and art; or rather, between the interests engaged by politics and the sentiments, perceptions, call them what you like, engaged by art. My reply, which I didn't quite succeed in making, was that he wanted to use art solely rather than to appreciate, enjoy or admire it, and to use it as an instrument of political change; that he wanted to give himself the feeling of achieving, through the experience of art, the social changes he and his companions had failed to bring about by direct political action or political rhetoric. I kept recalling, but not accurately enough to quote, a passage in Walter Benjamin's *Reflections* which seems to me decisive. I quote it now:

> If it is the double task of the revolutionary intelligentsia to over-throw the intellectual predominance of the bourgeoisie and to make contact with the proletarian masses, the intelligentsia has failed almost entirely in the second part of this task because it can no longer be performed contemplatively. And yet this has hindered hardly anybody from approaching it again and again as if it could, and calling for proletarian poets, thinkers, and artists. To counter this, Trotsky had to point out – as early as *Literature and Revolution* – that such artists would only emerge from a victorious revolution.

The TV programme ended, as usual, when a genuine argument seemed about to begin.

Now I want to approach the question from another direction.

At the Marquise de Saint-Euverte's, Swann heard again the phrase from Vinteuil's sonata for violin and piano. It was 'as if the musicians were not so much playing the little phrase as performing the rites necessary for its appearance'. A few pages later Proust reverts to the idiom of rites and ceremonies. It appears to Swann, thinking of Vinteuil, that 'the ineffable utterance of one solitary man, absent, perhaps dead . . . breathed out above the rites of those two hierophants, sufficed to arrest the attention of three hundred minds, and made of that stage on which a soul was thus called into being one of the noblest altars on which a supernatural ceremony could be performed.' The destiny of the phrase from the sonata is linked 'for the future with that of the human soul, of which it is one of the special, the most distinctive ornaments'.

Gilles Deleuze, in his *Proust et les signes*, points to that first sentence about the musicians performing the rites, and offers it as a motto for the spirituality of art in Proust. By spirituality he means the aspiration, which he ascribes to art itself as if it had desires corresponding to Proust's, toward a condition in which the work of art and its meaning are one. 'As long as we discover a sign's meaning in something else, matter still subsists, refractory to spirit.' Art, on the contrary, 'gives us the true unity: unity of an immaterial sign and of an entirely spiritual meaning.' Deleuze gives the name 'essence' to that 'unity of sign and meaning as it is revealed in the work of art'. It follows that 'the superiority of art over life consists in this; that all the signs we meet in life are still material signs, and their meaning, since it is always in something else, is not altogether spiritual.'

Essence is Deleuze's word for mystery. The implication of Proust's idiom of rites, ceremonies and altars is that art doesn't address problems, it acknowledges mystery. The dictionaries tell us that mystery, in Greek religion, refers to the secret religious ceremonies, such as those of Demeter at Eleusis, which were allowed to be witnessed only by initiates, sworn never to disclose their nature. In later Christian Greek, mystery refers to a sacrament, an outward sign of inward grace, especially the Eucharist. More generally, mystery is a truth offered only by divine revelation. Deleuze would prefer to talk of essence than of mystery, because essence is established as a more acceptable term in Western philosophy. Essence can then denote the aspiration, not only in Proust but in many other late nineteenth-century artists, toward the purest form of spirituality. If, as Pater thought, all the arts aspire to the condition of music, it is because music, or at least certain kinds of music, testifies to the possibility of Deleuze's 'unity of an immaterial sign and an entirely spiritual meaning'. Certain forms of dance, as in Mallarmé's *Hérodiade*, hold out the same possibility.

But Deleuze hasn't gone far into the question of a relation between essence and existence. Is essence a quality of existence, or at least of existence in certain forms? Or is it to be defined by its not being found in existence at all, by its being sustained only by a sense of its absence or its loss? Platonists nominate essence, and give it absolute privilege, so they are bound to represent everything in existence as fallen, imperfect, secondary. But there are other traditions. Santayana, especially in *Scepticism and Animal Faith* and *Three Philosophical Poets*, makes the world compatible with every desire we feel in its context and therefore reduces the distinction – mitigates it – between essence and existence. By an act of animal faith, he takes the world of matter for granted; he deals with it as an animal in the jungle deals with trees, he acts on the assumption that they are there. With the authority that each of us is, whatever else, a body, Santayana locates in the body of the world whatever truths we discover. 'Spirit' is his word for consciousness, but it is congenially practised in the living context of the world. According to him, we perceive appearances by a faculty he calls 'intuition'. The appearances themselves he calls essences; they receive their authority from our

24

certainty that they are, as appearances, exactly what they are. If I think I hear a certain sound, it is indisputable that I think I hear it. I may be in error as to the sound, but the question of error is another question, it does not refute the fact that I think I hear the sound. Santayana deals with the question of essence and existence by assimilating both terms to a realm of indisputable appearances: what appears to my intuition is indisputable as an appearance. In a state of extreme concentration, a mind can contemplate essences for themselves alone. Some of these may be embodied as appearances; some perhaps not. In that respect, as Kenneth Burke has pointed out, there are more essences than there are appearances.

If Proust finds essence in a work of art, and if, in Deleuze's terms, he defines essence as the unity of sign and meaning, his aesthetic is indeed spiritual. But Swann's isn't. Swann insists on domesticating the phrase from Vinteuil's sonata; he does not discover the meaning of the sign in itself, he does not acknowledge the union of sign and meaning. Instead, he prescribes the meaning of the sign as being somewhere else. At various times, he identifies the musical phrase with a woman, a woman's smile, someone who speaks to him of his beloved Odette, someone who carries past him his sorrows. He personifies the phrase so that his experience of it may be, to his own satisfaction, complete. At the Verdurins, when he hears it again, the personalising is extreme:

> More marvellous than any maiden, the little phrase, enveloped, arrayed in silver, glittering with brilliant sonorities, as light and soft as silken scarves, came to me, recognisable in this new guise. My joy at having rediscovered it was enhanced by the tone, so friendly and familiar, which it adopted in addressing me, so persuasive, so simple, and yet without subduing the shimmering beauty with which it glowed.

Such passages are handsome, one would not wish them away, but they show that Swann can only receive a sign by projecting something else as its meaning. He is in the same position as someone who, looking at a painting, reports to his friend that it reminds him of such-and-such a time. Proust's madeleine reminds him of Sunday mornings at Combray: there is no harm, no distortion, the madeleine is not a work of art. But Vinteuil's phrase reminds Swann of Odette: he personifies it to make the recollection complete. It is not that he resents its mystery, its spiritual unity, but that his need for other sentiments is more acute. His strongest justification, if the question were to arise, would be the fact that discourse, the habit of language, points him in that direction.

Deleuze's *Proust et les signes* provides a means of representing the two opposed sentiments in nineteenth-century art: the first, of those artists who were content to let the meaning of their signs be found elsewhere – as in the art of realism, or programme-music, official portraiture, or photographs, when they arrived, in which the content was everything and the composition nothing: and the second, according to which the sign itself would be found disgusting if it allowed its meaning to be discovered or projected elsewhere – we think of Mallarmé, the Symbolists, *l'Art pour l'Art*, Surrealism, and Cubism. The distinction is like the one Yeats made in 'The Trembling of the Veil' between writers who resorted to some propaganda or traditional doctrine to give them companionship with their fellows – he is thinking of Arnold, Browning, Tennyson, poets who held 'moral values that were not aesthetic values'; and, on the other side, those poets – Coleridge, Rossetti, the poets, too, of the 'Tragic Generation', who made 'what Arnold has called that "morbid effort", that search for "perfection of thought and feeling, and to unite this to perfection of form", poets who "sought this new, pure beauty, and suffered in their lives because of it".' Benjamin, an unlikely aspirant to such purity, nevertheless espoused it in the essay in which he praised the early direction of Surrealism:

> Life only seemed worth living where the threshold between waking and sleeping was worn away in everyone as by the steps of multitudinous images flooding back and forth, language only seemed itself where sound and image, image and sound interpenetrated with automatic precision and such felicity that no chink was left for the penny-in-the-slot called 'meaning'.

It is the sentiment here that is to the point, not the exaggerated praise of early Surrealism as bearer of the sentiment.

I have gone into the nineteenth-century phase of this sentiment mainly to enlarge the context in which an argument about politics and the arts might begin. A decent beginning is impossible so long as it is conducted, as Eagleton tried to conduct it, in terms of alleged elitism and authoritarianism. The crucial issue has to do with unity, and with the work of art as the image of that unity. The political issue can be raised, with a show of respectability, only in that setting.

It is well known that early twentieth-century criticism was preoccupied with a demand that the autonomy of the particular work of art be acknowledged. But what does a claim upon autonomy mean? It doesn't mean that the work of art is unrelated to anything and everything else in the world: such a claim is absurd. A valid claim means to say that the work of art cannot be reduced to its constituents; a novel cannot be reduced, for instance, to its story, plot, characters, and so forth. A sculpture cannot be reduced to the materials of which it is made. The autonomy of the work of art is embodied, therefore, in its precise form, its structure, however inadequately these terms may be construed. Early twentieth-century critics – the New Critics in literature, for instance – thought it important to define and defend the autonomy of the work of art because that autonomy testified to artistic creation as a special form of knowledge, a superior form. Critics argued among themselves in describing this difference. Some of them claimed that artistic knowledge was superior because more complete than any of the partial forms of knowledge professed by science, economics, or politics. Other critics claimed that artistic or poetic knowledge was superior because it embodied a different attitude to life, an attitude of reverence and appreciation rather than the predatory attitude embodied in other forms of knowledge. But in any case the achieved work of art was deemed to embody a far higher degree of unity than anything else in the world – unity, as in the Proustian sense described by Deleuze. The achieved work of art is present to itself, more fully at one with itself, than anything in the world which completes its meaning elsewhere, apart from its own form.

Terry Eagleton can't understand the sentiment which aspires to such unity; or indeed to any form of unity. He can only think of a work of art as a text of propaganda, a means to a political end. He can't understand why I emphasise the interrogative relation between a work of art and the society it, in some sense, addresses; because the only relation he understands is an instrumental relation. In my terms, a work of art exerts interrogative pressure on those who see it (read it; hear it; no matter) so far as it discloses, in its form, the highest possible achievement of itself as a free construction. In our time, reality is administered mostly by politics: the function of the arts is the critical interrogation of politics, the questioning of its certitudes. To the degree to which politics and management propose – or threaten – to live our lives for us; to that degree, the arts hold out the possibility of our remaining, in some sense and with at least some part of our conscious lives, independent. The interrogation is, of course, implicit; as we say that one set of terms questions another. The work of art does not question political rhetoric directly: its achieved presence – the degree of unity it achieves with itself – is a silent interrogation, in no respect disabled because of its silence.

A few days after the TV *Voices* debate, I took up Roberto Mangabeira Unger's book *Knowledge and Power*. One chapter of that book addresses, in connexion with a theory of the self, the question of politics and art. Unger's purpose does not coincide with mine, but his argument is helpful. He starts with the fact that 'everyday life is given over to the profane, the prosaic, and the rule of self-interest', hence 'the sacred, art, and love appear as extraordinary deviations'. The extraordinary representation of the ideal in art, religion, and love has, he continues, a certain significance for everyday life. On the one hand, 'it can offer the self temporary refuge': the very availability of the ideal makes its absence from everyday life seem tolerable. Precisely 'because the sacred, art and love are separated out from banal events', these events 'can proceed all the more relentlessly in their profane, prosaic, and self-regarding way.' However, 'the extraordinary also makes it possible to grasp the ideal, and to contrast it with one's ordinary experience of the world.' In this sense, 'the extraordinary is the starting point for the critique and transformation of social life': it poses for people 'the task of actualising in the world of commonplace things and situations what they have already encountered as a divine liberation from the everyday.'

Unger argues that there are two errors to be avoided. The first is to disregard 'the link between the development of the individual self and the situation of society': if you cut the tie between consciousness and politics, you present the ideal of the self as something that can only be realised in the private life, 'and whose attainment is independent of society.' The second error is to insist that 'if the ideal of the self can be realised at all it must be realised politically and in history.' This position 'fails to account for those phenomena of individual consciousness that do not seem peculiar to any one historical situation': its moral implication is 'to deny that private and extraordinary experience can ever, to any extent, actualise the ideal of the self'. Unger would maintain that while human nature shows itself 'only through the historical forms of social organisation and social consciousness', it is not exhausted or completely determined by any of them.

Unger's argument strikes me as far more fruitful than Eagleton's, and, in the best sense, far more liberal. I welcome the fact that his terms for the good are drawn from the extraordinary, his word for such experiences as those of religion, art, and love, and that these terms are to be brought to bear upon everyday life. I don't see any difficulty in reconciling this view with my sense of the arts as interrogation. The criteria are found in the work of art, fulfilled in whatever degree one's critical judgement suggests; these are then brought to bear upon the procedures of daily life.

My only reservation, in thinking of Unger's position, is that he underestimates the extent to which one's sense of the extraordinary in religion, art, and love is blunted by the discursive processes which accompany it and govern, in one degree or another, its reception at large. Unger speaks as if one's access to the extraordinary were entirely a matter of one's individual disposition: it is not.

TWO
THE DOMESTICATION OF OUTRAGE

It's hard, these days, to feel outrage. When the Argentinian army took possession of South Georgia and the Falkland Islands, many people felt that it was outrageous, but I think too that they were consoled to discover that they could still feel this emotion. Mary Whitehouse has made a public life for herself by specialising in outrage; not so much by collecting instances of the outrageous as by alerting herself to the sense of it, keeping it going when it would otherwise have lapsed; as it has lapsed in most people. The plain fact is that bourgeois society can accommodate nearly anything. I should say, incidentally, that I use the word 'bourgeois' as a neutral term and often a term of praise, though one is supposed to use it nowadays only for irony or contempt. To me a bourgeois liberal is one who bases his liberalism upon a commitment to the values of a family man, anxious to secure a decent future for his children. A bourgeois society approves these values and regards the occasions on which they are defeated as regrettable. A bourgeois criticism of art likes to report that images which seem wild or bizarre are not really different from the ordinary images with which we are familiar. Such criticism likes to take part in 'the rapid domestication of the outrageous' which Leo Steinberg has named as the most typical feature of contemporary artistic life.

The artistic attempts made from time to time to outrage people are hapless. We wouldn't expect much from nine-minute wonders, like Mary Kelly's display of used nappy liners or Victor Burgin's stapled photographs. But more consequential artists find it hard to stir the sense of the appalling. Diane Arbus's photographs may have been taken to remind people that thousands of lives are broken, thousands of bodies crippled, that there are people who seem to have no life but the horror of it. But when you look through a book of Arbus's photographs, you feel that what they make is a freak-show. The feeling is a temporary aberration from normality which reinforces our sense of what is normal, like the experience most people will have had on going to see *The Elephant Man*.

The most telling consequence of the domestication of outrage is that far from disturbing the security of ordinary things, it confirms it. You can make an interesting photograph of anything, however commonplace. Long before Pop Art, photography broke down the distinction between the features of art and the features of ordinary life: for that reason, it was a long time before it was taken seriously as anything more than a device for recalling large occasions.

The difference between photography and the older tradition of the still life in painting is that photography, being technological, found it easy to deal with machine-made shapes. The camera turned everything, natural or manufactured, into a image, and asked you to look hard at the result. But a photograph of a car is not a car; just as there is a difference between a car and the word 'car'. The mysteriousness of art is in all art, not merely in the art of the avant garde; it suffuses the space between the image and its reference. The difference between a great painting and the materials from which it is made is finally mysterious; 'finally' in the sense that much can be said about the painting before reaching the point at which you have to leave it to silence. But mystery is not a secret message which the critic, in principle, could discover. There are many things to be said about Brancusi's sculpture 'Endless Column', for instance, but nothing useful can be said about it on the assumption that it has a meaning it could be persuaded to disclose, or that any such meaning would exhaust it.

What remains hidden is the presence of the work, the force of its presence as distinct from the particular bits of bronze or marble or whatever it's made of. There are works of art which are present to us in something like the way in which a person may be present to us. When you love people, you don't assess their qualities, you acknowledge them without thinking of reasons or thinking that any reason would matter. So it's entirely proper to speak of loving a work of art since we extend the word from our use of it in personal life. Or at least that's a way of recognising and celebrating what I have called its presence. The reason why modern critics are embarrassed by the mysteriousness of art is that it threatens the purity of their secular status. My evidence for this isn't particular critics but the techniques they use, the confidence they place in their sentences. They insist upon the assurance that nothing escapes their consciousness. If they sense that the work of art is indeed occult, they get away from it as quickly as possible. They keep going till they reach the artist. This displacement of interest from the work of art to the artist is nearly incorrigible.

John Berger has pointed out that the artist is no longer valued as the producer of his work, but instead for the quality of his vision and imagination as expressed in it. No longer primarily a maker of art, he is 'an example of a man, and it is his art which exemplifies him'. Now that's true, even though the work of art may command a high price.

If an artist is admired or cherished, it is for what he is, an instance of a certain kind of person. But he's also valued because he enables us to feel that we are in touch with art by seeing the artist. The resentment against mystery is mostly against its absolute difference from ourselves. It's difficult to say anything about Hans Ulrich Lehmann's 'Duets for Three Players'; it is an unwelcoming work, so the critic goes off to Lehmann himself, who turns out to be, so far as appearance is evidence, a man like any other. He can be a little different but not very different. What is unusual appears only in his music and not in the image we see of him.

Once on the safe ground of the artist, the critic uses any of a number of available terminologies of explanation. One of the most popular at the moment is psychoanalysis: writers such as Freud, Melanie Klein, and Lacan have provided an official vocabulary, a relatively easy set of categories, quite limited in number, at least one of which the artist may be expected to fulfil. In a recent exploit, a critic proposed to explain Henry James's work on the basis of his having been passionately in love with his brother William. James's biographer Leon Edel was so taken with this notion that he undertook to read James's entire fiction again in this light: his implication was that the new reading would be far more profound than the old one. In fact, there is no objection to the application of psychoanalytic concepts to a work of art except that the exercise seems doomed to be reductive.* The psychology of the artist seeks to know him not as a special case but as an unusually clear manifestation of the ordinary. The artist is now deemed to be unusual only because he provides more evidence than other people. To be fair, any established terminology is bound to reduce its object; that is its purpose, to make sense of an obscurity by bringing to bear upon it the sense that has already been made in another way. Psychoanalysis is a dialect, a choice of privileged concepts within a language – it has the character of diction

*Gaston Bachelard's form of psychoanalysis may appear to make an exception to this statement; but it doesn't. His books are not psychoanalytical characterisations of artists; they are studies of the sentiments provoked by the elements, fire, space, water, and so forth.

in poetry, a set of favourite words which are brought together for mutual support. But the trouble with the psychoanalytical interpretation of art is that it interprets not art but the artist: in that sense it's bound to evade the question of mystery or otherness.

Adrian Stokes, for instance, following Melanie Klein's theory about the way in which a young child's mind is formed, thought of the subject-matter of art as dominated by two experiences that have been internalised: the feeling of oneness with the mother's breast and therefore with the world; and secondly, the recognition of a separation between the child and the world, originally the mother's whole person whose loss was mourned.* For Stokes, the artistic motive is the need to restore the lost loved object. He then distinguishes two forms of this motive: first, 'a very strong indentification with the object whereby a barrier between self and not-self is undone'; and second, 'a commerce with a self-sufficient and independent object at arm's length'.§

*Mourned in the infantile depressive position. The infant incorporates the mother's breast as a 'good object' but, in the scene of frustration, having projected on to the breast his own rage, he incorporates a 'bad object' too.

Now Stokes's psychoanalytic theory of art is useful. His distinction between the two forms of the artistic motive could be applied, for instance, to the experience of looking at a painting. First we try to break down the barrier between us: at a later stage we may draw back from it and try to judge it, and to do this we have to take the painting as an independent object at arm's length. But the trouble with Stokes's theory, when he applies it to particular works of art and architecture, is that the works are called upon merely to confirm the theory. If you took the theory as strictly as Stokes took it, you might still know a lot about art but you would have only one way of knowing it. And you would be so rigorous in confirming the same few axioms that you might fail to see the differences between one work of art and another. His discourse makes certain perceptions possible, but it's also restrictive, it prevents you from perceiving what lies beyond it or to one side of it.

§This distinction is then developed into one between carving and modelling in sculpture: it is Stokes's most influential distinction, and immensely valuable. In a letter to The Listener, 16 December 1982, Richard Read rebuked me for citing Stokes to exemplify what I had in mind here. He quoted, from The Invitation in Art, Stokes's objection to 'the easy atomising of the patently imaginative' promoted by certain kinds of psychoanalytical argument. I accept the rebuke.

The work of art is seen as the artist's way of dealing with compulsions which he treated otherwise when he was a child, by turning to the breast. The compulsions themselves are unconscious, but the theory accounts for them by telling a plausible story. And because a story takes place in time, it brings into time and rationality factors which otherwise would have little chance of getting there. Critics who want to escape from the mysteriousness of the work try to replace it by the intention they ascribe to the artist. Some works of art make this procedure necessary. A few years ago Robert Klein argued that it is no longer possible to judge a painting or sculpture without knowing who made it and in what spirit.

When we look at a contemporary painting in a gallery, we search for the artist's name and the title of the painting, if it has one. We do this not out of mere helplessness or curiosity but in the hope of seeing the work as the fulfilment of an intention. If we know the artist, we may happen to know his general line: if so, all the better. What Klein meant, I think, was that the work of art now persists chiefly as an indication of an intention; it is as an embodied intention that it can best be studied. We are led straight from the work to the psychology of the artist and from there to the economics of the market. To be blunt: it pays to deliver certain recognisable objects and intentions. It is comforting to be in the presence of intentions we understand because the considerations of psychology and economics aren't at all mysterious: discussion of them is easy.

The question sometimes arises whether the work exceeds the intention or merely documents it. You'll recall the incident, a few years ago, when the Tate Gallery paid good domestic cash for a work called 'Equivalent VIII', a load of bricks laid on the floor by the artist Carl Andre. Andre's intention was far more interesting than the bricks or the order in which he assembled them. He explained it in a conversation, a few months ago, with Edward Lucie-Smith. Referring to Turner's way with colour, he said that Turner had severed colour from depiction and then manipulated it in a condition of freedom. 'I sever matter from depiction,' he said. 'I am the Turner of matter.' He meant that in choosing bricks, metal plates, or bales of hay, he chooses things that are associated with particular uses, and he diverts them from those uses so that he can give them intrinsic existence.* Andre's intention is to assert that art is a system of pleasure, based chiefly upon our physical presence in a material world. It's like the theory of literature put forward by the Russian critic Boris Shklovsky, that the function of literature is to free things of their familiarity so that we can really perceive them, looking at them as if they were strange.

> *Andre's materials have not already become what their manufacturer wanted them finally to be: as, for instance, a car-mirror (Joseph Beuys) or a lavatory seat (Duchamp).

Normally we look at things mainly for their use; we deal with them as we deal with the wallpaper in our rooms, we would notice it only if it were gone, torn, or daubed with paint. Carl Andre wants much the same result. Looking at his bricks, we see them as such, as objects: the artist has forced us to pay attention. He doesn't claim that there is anything sacred in the bricks themselves, or even in his way of disposing them.

Andre regards the artistic event as a combination of the artist's intention and our way of receiving it. Is there anything against this? No, except that art in this sense can have no history other than that of its intention. Once we have taken the point and resolved to amend our lives accordingly, there is nothing more to do. Like any one of Andy Warhol's films, it is not necessary to see it, it's enough to understand that it is there, and why. In that respect, unfortunately, the comparison with Turner doesn't hold.

Up to this point the displacement of attention from the work of art to the artistic life sounds innocent. If the work sits there, retaining its mystery, returning our stare, why shouldn't we turn aside to consult the artist, who is more likely to answer whatever questions a common discourse allows us to ask? Can't we go back to the work at any time and renew our sense of its occult power? Yes, but in practice one interest has displaced the other, precisely because an interest in the artist is easily satisfied. And there is a further consideration. Increasingly, the form in which we pay attention to anything is a result of the way in which we watch images on television. We pay attention to most things now as if they were television programmes.* Now television is restless with any object which asks to be looked at slowly and patiently. The span of willing attention to an image on television is a matter of seconds, not minutes. Then a new image must be given. When such programmes as *Omnibus* and *The South Bank Show* present an artist, they run away from his works and concentrate on him, an easier subject because he is responsive, mobile, unsecretive. Instead of a work of art to be looked at, the camera gives us a man or woman, much like anybody else, so we are not affronted by seeing anything strikingly different from ourselves. Objects, when presented at all, are turned into happenings. A

*I am not 'attacking' television, as several people who work in television jumped to conclude. But television provides two experiences which are, in the end, soothing: the displacement of one image by another; and the sentiment of being together, all of us, sharing these images and the reality they are supposed to constitute.

recent *South Bank Show* about Sir William Walton said nothing about the character or the principles of his music, but plenty about the kind of man he was. It may be that people who watched the programme have been so stimulated by the personal lore it provided that they have gone straight to his music. I can't be certain, but I doubt it. And even if it were true, it still wouldn't have provoked the right sort of attention, because they would receive the music as further illustration of a personal image.

In T.S. Eliot's *The Elder Statesman* Lord Claverton discovers that he's been freed, at last, 'from the self that pretends to be someone'. 'And in becoming no one,' he finds, 'I begin to live.' He begins to live, and to live in a social world, because he has given up all pretence: his privacy is not a secret self behind his disclosed appearances. But television has got people into the habit of assuming that what is there begins and ends with what they see.

The same process takes over the presentation of art. Hence the fact that the most famous artists in our time are famous as personalities rather than as makers of their works.* This doesn't mean that, like Bianca Jagger, they are famous for being famous. They are artists, they have made things – pictures, films, songs. But the images they offer to the public gaze are more compelling than the works they have made. Think of Salvador Dali.

> **Hilary Mills has argued, in her biography of Norman Mailer, that Mailer's personality is already more compelling than his works.*

Most people recall a crucifixion, liquefied watches, popular reproductions in the postcard-shops. But Dali's form of existence before the world has made him a personality far more visible than his paintings. Allen Ginsberg became a symbol even for people who couldn't name one of his poems. Andy Warhol is far more famous as a personality than as a painter or a film director; he exists as a gesture, a snapshot from the album of the Sixties. His fame persists not because it corresponds to any new work he has done but because many people now approaching middle age feel nostalgic toward the decade in which they felt that they were making history. Warhol reminds them of that sentiment. It's not necessary that he should ever take up a paintbrush again.§

> *§Other phenomena: John Lennon, far more famous than any of his songs, now that the manner of his death has increased the disproportion between his life and his*

This disproportion between artist and his work – the fact that with the connivance of the media a little work goes a long way to sustain a personality – marks a reversal of the traditional relation between the two. It was long thought a sign of success in an artist that

37

he disappeared into his work, leaving no merely personal residue. Henry James thought that this made it extremely difficult to write a novel about a successful artist; there was not enough left over, everything had gone into the work. 'Any presentation of the artist *in triumph*,' he said, 'must be flat in proportion as it really sticks to its subject – it can only smuggle in relief and variety. For, to put the matter in an image, all we then – in his triumph – see of the charm-compeller is the back he turns to us as he bends over his work.' James felt that the good fortune of an artist would be to remain anonymous, visible in his works and not otherwise; and that his being also a person should be a matter of his privacy and reserve.

work; Elvis Presley, whose career makes it easy to attach to a creature of the media the sentiments appropriate to loss and waste.

But we have now reached a situation in which privacy and reserve can be converted to visible purpose. The fact that Philip Larkin doesn't appear on television and rarely gives readings of his poetry has added to his fame. His invisibility has become a nuance of visibility. A *South Bank Show* on Larkin turned his absence into an esoteric form of presence.★

★ *. . . like Graham Greene appearing in a TV programme only to the extent of the back of his head, his voice, and – am I right in recalling? – his hands.*

The urgency with which critics run from the work of art to the artist is only partly explained by the fact that the work remains mysterious and the artist doesn't. There is also undisguised revulsion against the sacred object, the original work of art. Photography is a comfortable medium because even if you see photographs which are also works of art, you're not browbeaten by their sublimity; such works are extraordinary examples of the ordinary rather than works of genius, like *King Lear*, which no one in his senses could dream that he might write. But the unique work of art is intimidating. Think of the depression of spending more than an hour in an art gallery. The aura that surrounds a masterpiece is the sign of its uniqueness, it attends our sense that there is only one of it and that any likeness is only a replica. This consideration gives the unique work its prestige, and not only in Sotheby's, but it is also the focus of a vague resentment. Few of us would really want to own a masterpiece, it would be out of place in our homes. We are happier with decent colour-reproductions, because they don't intimidate, we don't feel oppressed by them. Lithographs are acceptable because there is no orginal; they are all equal.

There is also a political explanation for this, asserted most vigorously by Marxist critics. Walter Benjamin has observed that history is always recited in favour of those who have won; the point of view of the defeated is never recorded. 'As in all previous history,' he says, 'whoever emerges as victor still participates in that triumph in which today's rulers march over the prostrate bodies of their victims. As is customary, the spoils are borne aloft in that triumphal parade. These are generally called the cultural heritage. There has never been a document of culture which was not at one and the same time a document of barbarism.' Benjamin's argument shouldn't make you feel guilty when you go to a gallery or a museum. For one thing, if the victors in a particular society were workers rather than princes, there is no reason to think that their triumph would be achieved and maintained without victims. A triumphal parade would still take place. One has only to attend a 'first night' in the West End or at Lincoln Center to feel that the event, whatever its artistic occasion, is also a celebration of victory. The happy few are on display to themselves and to one another.

One has the same misgiving on going to see the Kennedy Center for the Performing Arts in Washington. The building has transformed cultural life in that city, but it stands as an architectural assertion of the imperial motives that built it. Domination is inscribed in its marble. Richard Hoggart has recently asserted, following the conventional wisdom on such matters, that there is 'an almost total loss of confidence in the very idea of a higher culture to which one could and should aspire'. I would want to put it differently. Certainly the idea of accredited values, known and accepted as such whether an individual aspires to them or not, has broken down. The idea of aspiration, in anything but a careerist sense, has lapsed. But the Sydney Opera House, the new Barbican, and Kennedy Center are still making assertions in favour of cultural life, even if the assertions come from an equivocal mixture of power, national pride, and a commitment to continuity. The loss of confidence has occurred, not in the decisiveness with which these buildings are built, but in knowing what should be produced in them, once they are built. What is desperately confused is the relation between cultural life and its components: the break in the circuit of attention between the work of art, the artist, the critic, and the common reader, listener or viewer is only one sign of that confusion.

It may seem that the drift or the flight from the work of art to the artist is refuted by at least one contemporary form of criticism. Structuralists and post-Structuralists maintain that the notion of the author as the creator of his works is merely a modern consolation prize; it goes along with the prestige a bourgeois society ascribes to the individual. Roland Barthes and other critics regard as mere superstition any attempt to find the depth of the work in the psyche of the author. Instead, they replace the author by language itself, which is then studied as an impersonal system, a system that doesn't need a person to work it. The idea is that language allows for a personal intervention in the moment of writing or speaking, but the person ceases with the enunciation: nothing in language corresponds to the identity of a person or to his apparent continuity from one moment to the next. The author is at best a secretary, a scribe.

But the Structuralist thesis doesn't attribute any mystery to language as a system of signs. A critic who is interested in modern literature is not supposed to deal with it as acts of the creative imagination in the medium of a particular language. He is supposed to find that the work of art is a mere function of a compromised language, corrupted because it has been used in the exercise of power and on behalf of an ideology. The job of criticism is to document the extent to which the modern languages have been corrupted.

In turn, Structuralist readers are urged to adopt an ironic or sceptical attitude toward whatever they read; they are to know that it is poisoned. Barthes, in his later work, showed how such readers might behave themselves. They should cultivate caprice and excess, going against the grain of the writing, distrusting its rhetorical figures, reading at their own speed. In this way they retain some measure of freedom, and break the conspiracy between author, publisher, and the economy of the market which has produced the book as a commodity for sale.

It begins to appear that in Structuralism and post-Structuralism we are returned to something like the avant-garde position in relation to a society deemed to be bourgeois through and through. No wonder critics who start with these assumptions about the impersonality of language tend to lose interest in criticism and to become writers, as if to fill the avant-garde position left vacant by novelists and poets.

I often wish the Structuralists were right. It would be pleasant to give up the sense of mystery in the arts and to think that everything in the work could be explained in systematic terms. The French critics want to get rid of mystery because it sounds like theology or divinity. But I am not persuaded. The idea of a language as a system explains everything in a work of literature except what we most have to acknowledge; on that, the idea is helpless. It's at this point, and against the Structuralists, that we have to reinstate the artist: indeed, it's extraordinary that it should be necessary to say that he is the one who has made the work. What do we gain by saying that T.S. Eliot's 'Gerontion' is a work of language, or even of the English language, and that Eliot is merely its scribe? The point about a scribe is that someone else could do his work. To refuse to call the writing of 'Gerontion' a creative act performed with the collaboration of the English language is nonsense. The fact that the English language is a communal creation, the work of its speakers over many centuries, is not at all incompatible with the creative imagination we ascribe to Eliot in this instance. A linguistic system makes certain things possible, but it makes nothing actual. Nothing could ever be done if it were left to a system to do it.

Commentary

What I said about bourgeois liberalism, liberal humanism, the middle class, and so forth gave offence to some listeners. I am unrepentant. Hostility to bourgeois society has become a cliché, an unearned symbol of spiritual superiority. More to the point: some listeners maintained that I contradicted myself. In one lecture I was speaking up for bourgeois liberalism; in another, insisting that the artistic stance must be interrogative, even subversive.

There is no contradiction. In *Culture and Anarchy* Matthew Arnold presented a typology of the three recognised social classes of England – aristocracy, middle class, and working class – as Barbarians, Philistines, and Populace. According to this typology, he was himself a Philistine. But he also allowed for the existence, within each class, of a number of aliens, men and women who, although classifiable as members of one class or another, wore their typology with a difference: 'Persons who are mainly led, not by their class spirit, but by a general *humane* spirit, by the love of human perfection.' Those people would have a better chance of recognising and pursuing their 'best self' than anyone who coincided at all points with his class and its typical interests. Those people, too, would play a particularly leading part in the work of what Arnold called, prudently or not, Culture.

It may be felt that the precedent is too grand for the occasion. But it seems necessary, misunderstanding being what it is, to invoke strong authority to align oneself with a general social position while keeping the alignment incomplete. I am under no obligation to approve of everything a bourgeois society does or of every interest it pursues. As a matter of demonstrable fact, however, I could make a far better case for the sentiments and actions normally considered bourgeois than my colleagues in literary and social criticism appear ready to make; even if the terms of the enquiry were agreed to turn upon questions of power and justice, poverty, 'the wretched of the earth'. I am a member of the middle class; in some respects I coincide with its official interest, in other respects I am an alien within it. When I propose an interrogative or subversive stance for the arts in relation to societies mainly bourgeois, I think it important that certain intuitions and sentiments be kept alive which are not, or at least not as a regular thing, maintained by those societies. Not precisely 'when in Rome, do as the Greeks', but 'when in Rome, think, feel, and imagine as the Greeks'.

On the question of reductiveness: I didn't say that all psychoanalytical criticism is reductive; but that any such criticism that concerns itself with the artist rather than the work of art is reductive. Many other kinds of criticism, too, are reductive; criticism that diverts attention – without making it clear that attention is indeed being diverted – from the work to the life of the artist, his biography, his historical circumstances, and so forth. Some of these forms of criticism may indeed send us back to the works themselves. The poet Harvey Shapiro told me, a few months ago, that Richard Ellmann's biography of Joyce had this effect on him. Splendid: but I suspect that for many readers Ellmann's *Joyce* – the life, the detail – has virtually replaced Joyce's own work, and appeased in advance the interests a reading of the work, from *Dubliners* to *Finnegans Wake*, would otherwise fulfil.

Of course it is easier to read a big biography of an artist than to engage directly with his works. The popularity of biographies, by comparison with the chilly welcome normally given to works of criticism, is easily explained. But the explanation should also refer to the common desire to find the 'perfection of the work', in Yeats's phrase, elucidated in relation to the imperfection of the artist's life. There seems to be a special pleasure in discovering, for instance, that the author of *Ulysses* and *Finnegans Wake* was a commonplace man as well as a genius. Or in any case, that the hauteur of the fiction, the force with which it guards its mystery, can be resolved into the commonplaces of the life.

A second thought. An imaginary listener may have said: 'Would it not be possible to give a more congenial account of the reception of the arts in our society if you replaced your characterisation of it by a narrative?' Meaning this: what about the several accounts of reading, listening, and so on, which recognise that there are differences, of kind and degree, between one reader (listener, viewer) and another; differences that can be attributed to variations in education, experience, priorities of interest?

I want to pursue this further. Two texts occur to me. The first is an early essay by John Crowe Ransom on 'Freud and Literature'. Ransom maintains that while a work of literature becomes a public property as soon as it is uttered, it becomes such a thing differently in the hands of 'the many' and 'the few'.

> It may be that we should be too exacting of literature if we required
> that it should never intimidate the people by its difficulty, but

certainly we are in our rights in requiring that it must never affront them with an attack upon their morality. And so the fable, the obvious meaning of literature, lies on the surface to be easily appropriated by the people; but the initiated, according to their several degrees of advancement in the mysteries, can find further meanings suitable to their need, and these become more and more esoteric. Literature emulates the Apostle in attempting to be all things to all men, nor are men ever too humble to be the proper objects of its interest. And since the humblest must have their access as well as the greatest, literature becomes a study in indirection: its highest meaning, which is generally unsuitable for popular use, is discoverable but not manifest, and nowhere by its unconventionality does it flout what the orator terms 'the moral sensibilities of decent men'.

There is more of Ransom's high prose, but this is enough for now.

Some parts of the passage are not our concern: they arose, I think, from arguments Ransom was engaged in with his Southern associates about *The Waste Land* and other works of Modernism. The part I need is his recognition that 'the people' are to be distinguished from 'the initiated' in their approach to the arts. Incidentally, the charge of elitism doesn't arise: it would arise only if Ransom were to condemn 'the people' to their popular state as if by definition and as punishment for their ignorance or simplicity; or if he were to prescribe that entry to the condition of 'the initiated' be limited to people of high breeding or some other quality that could not be acquired by effort. If it is granted that Ransom's distinction between the people and the initiated is not categorical but merely an observation of the facts of the case, and true as an observation; then there can be no objection to it.

It may appear that I should be content with Ransom's formulation. Hasn't he acknowledged 'the mysteries' and implied an Eleusinian reverence for them? Yes, but I can't approve his version of the distance between the people and the initiated in terms of 'meanings', more and more 'esoteric', until at last, presumably, the 'highest meaning' of the work, discoverable but not manifest, is indeed discovered. I would want a sense of the mystery of the work of art to pervade anyone's experience of it, at whatever degree of naïveté or initiation; and not as something to be dispelled by superior education or concentration of mind and purpose.

The second text is interestingly continuous with the first: it is the first chapter of Frank Kermode's *The Genesis of Secrecy*, where he distinguishes, in interpretation or hermeneutics, between the carnal and the spiritual sense of a text. The distinction is an old one, except for its diction: it is well established as distinguishing between the manifest sense of a text and a latent sense available only to the elect. The manifest sense of a story is what everyone makes of it, more or less; the latent sense is what someone on the inside makes of it. Or it might denote a distinction between an ordinary, straightforward gloss and an act of divination: the gloss would arise from a supposition that the story is nothing more than what it appears to be, the act of divination would arise from the supposition that the story is in some way oracular, yielding its sense not now but later or never. The agent of divination is the insider; the other is the outsider. The insider lives within the circle, the fellowship, the institution, where the score is known; the outsider is content with rougher satisfactions.

Kermode gives, as an example of manifest-reading, a straightforward account of Henry Green's *Party Going*, a story of young people travelling and failing to travel. The manifest sense goes no further than an account of the plot and a description of the main characters. Then he gives a latent reading of it, making much of pigeons and other strangers, the sort of thing an outsider wouldn't notice or, if he did, wouldn't make much sense of.

It may be asked: isn't Kermode's argument merely Ransom's, writ large and at length? But not quite: the difference is that Ransom doesn't say who the people are or who the initiated; they may not correspond exactly to Kermode's outsiders and insiders, or to 'the common reader' and the academic teacher. Kermode's interpreters are either inside the university, or not: a professional barrier, with its attendant rituals and rules, separates them. Also: Kermode's idiom of the carnal and the spiritual distinguishes between flesh, which each of us has, and spirit, which – to put the matter delicately – we do not all possess in equal measure.

Still, even with these differences in place, I would quarrel with Kermode on one issue: he assumes, as Ransom did, that there is nothing beyond the grasp of interpretive skill. He allows, indeed, for multiple discoveries; spiritual readings tend to be different, carnal readings tend to be the same. But presumably that is because each member of the elect is jealous of the precise character of his spirituality. We are all ready to assent to our bodily condition; any one of us might prefer to have a more beautiful body, but not to be bodiless. No one wants his spirit to be the same as his neighbour's. It is his insistence upon a spiritual difference that prompts Mallarmé to refer, in 'Le Mystère dans les Lettres' to 'la vaine couche suffisante d'intelligibilité'.

Kermode would probably allow that it is possible for an outsider to become an insider. The Christian instruction to priests, 'Go ye therefore, teach ye all nations', would have no point, otherwise; even apart from the consideration that vacancies in the elect must be filled. But he assumes, throughout *The Genesis of Secrecy*, that everything is a message, and that the difficulties of deciphering these messages are merely difficulties. I don't believe that everything is a message or a sign.

Is there any authority for this? I think of Wallace Stevens's poem 'Of Mere Being', its first lines:

The palm at the end of the mind,
Beyond the last thought, rises
In the bronze decor,
A gold-feathered bird
Sings in the palm, without human meaning,
Without human feeling, a foreign song.

(Some texts have 'distance' in place of 'decor' in the third line.)

Many of Stevens's poems urge us to believe that there is nothing at the end of the mind, that the mind is capable of going to whatever end there is. But this one seems to say that when the mind has exhausted itself, life in some form exceeds it. I have been persuaded by James Guetti's *Word-Music* that in many of Stevens's poems, including this one, the exhaustion of the reasoning power seems to be 'an exercise of mind that readies us to participate in a different sort of perception and energy'. This does not involve the familiar distinction between reason and imagination, as if reason were a work-horse and imagination a more spirited animal ready to take over when the drudge-work is done. The poem would be trivial if it merely said that when reason flags the imagination saves the day. The process is rather one in which the mind – call it reason or imagination for the moment, it doesn't matter – spends itself entirely; so that if anything rises in the world after that exhaustion, it rises independently of the mind and therefore truly is, embodies the being of the world, of life itself. Stevens's end, as Guetti beautifully describes it, 'is not intelligence achieved but spent – spent to prepare and allow the uprising of things arresting beyond our intelligence of them'.

46

And yet, and yet . . . what is Stevens doing, then, letting his phrases contradict what his mere sentence has asserted? The palm at the end of the mind: that is as close as Stevens's language can come to strict denotation. 'Rises' completes the sentence in much the same spirit. But then he sets a bird singing in the palm: singing, as if he wanted to subvert his sentence by alluding to Keats and Yeats and their singing birds, which sing incorrigibly of human feeling. 'Without human meaning,/ Without human feeling, a foreign song.' But no matter how foreign the song is said to be; if it is song, the word itself dissolves its foreignness. We come back to Cioran's sentence: 'The indigence of language renders the universe intelligible.' Is there a disjunction between Stevens's language, which insists on going one way, and his sentiment, which wants to go the opposite way? There must have been a lot of his feeling urging him in one direction if it took three nearly synonymous assertions to counter it. Assertion, followed by misgiving: say too much, then move back from the position you have taken.

Finally (for the moment) a word about Structuralism. It is hard to find anyone these days who would call himself a Structuralist, but I felt that the sentiment I described in this second lecture is still at large, and that its reductive bias should be mentioned. It is not news that some people who called themselves Structuralists a few years ago now call themselves post-Structuralists; or that the most damaging scrutiny of Structuralism has come from within its fellowship. I have quoted several passages of this scrutiny – many from Jacques Derrida – in my *Ferocious Alphabets*. Enough is (nearly) enough.

THREE

THE PARADE OF IDEAS

We cultivate, these days, a merely spectacular relation to ideas and attitudes: we watch them as they pass, as in a Lord Mayor's parade. They hold our interest while they stay in sight, but we're not committed to any of them. The same predicament arises in the reception of the arts. There's no longer a discourse, an accepted frame of reference and definition, which would enable us to know whether we agree or disagree on a particular matter. The words we use in criticism are obviously ideological and compromised, they are not neutral.★ Words which sound innocent, like tone, form, action and scene are just as argumentative as words like revolution, history, praxis and dialectic. You know a critic by the words he uses, but knowing him doesn't mean that you can easily talk to him. The words he uses enforce judgements already made by others, so there is no moment at which you could begin a conversation free of bias. The pluralist way of dealing with the built-in commitment of words is to think of them all ironically, to engage in a play of mind which ranges over them all with equal nonchalance. So we hear words like 'beauty' and 'truth' as if they had inverted commas around them. But the play of mind doesn't make available even the possibility of a shared understanding of the object: it's an act of power, not of communication. All you can do with a play of mind is to watch its performance.

One of the peculiar things about the present situation is that while the dialects of criticism have become more than ever divisive, the arts as an institution have been drawn into the general purposes of society. The first consequence is that democratic habits of mind, such as the objection to privilege, have provided, for

★*I take ideology to mean the deployment of a social rhetoric as if it were a force of nature and therefore irrefutable. Or: the masking of one's interest as verifiable knowledge. Alastair MacIntyre has argued, convincingly, that the reason why there is no rational means of achieving agreement on moral issues – on abortion, for instance, or nuclear policy – is that the concepts of moral argument we use 'were originally at home in larger totalities of theory and practice, contexts which gave the concepts their stability and meaning.' We are still trying to reach moral consensus by using conceptual fragments broken off from several*

better and worse, the conditions for the reception of | *incommensurate moral tradi-*
the arts. For better, because recourse to the arts is no | *tions and authorities.*
longer quite the exotic matter it was. Music, literature,
architecture and sculpture in public spaces make aesthetic experiences
widely available. For worse, because one of the vices of democracy is that
it tolerates mediocrity, especially if, as is the case now, mediocrity has a
large following. We are capable of putting up with it mainly because we
try to ignore it. Any expression of disgust for kitsch is neutralised, it's
deemed to be yet another mark of the unearned superiority of the
political Right or Left. Those who dissociate themselves from trash are
nullified by being turned into personalities: Malcolm Muggeridge, Kings-
ley Amis, William F. Buckley, John Osborne. When John Osborne reviews
a television show, nobody takes him seriously, he is merely exhibiting his
personality, and the readiness of such people to be turned into personalities gives concern for standards several bad names: elitism, spleen,
vanity.

It's a commonplace that people all over the world are tending to
become the same, even where there are apparent differences of race,
creed, and tradition. And it's true, I think, that power in our time is
exercised mostly for the production of the same images. The best that
can be said for pluralism is that it doesn't kill people or torture them or
even suppress them. After that, it lets people have the feeling of being
different on the silent understanding that they will gradually, in any
case, conform to the same. Nietzsche said that the motive of art is to be
different, to be elsewhere. Presumably he meant to be different not only
from other people but from one's ordinary self.

It may appear that I am invoking a 'spirit of the age' without having
established the merit of doing so. Since Hegel, we have been encouraged
to assume that the age has a spirit, an inner mark or character which it
utters in various ways. It's hard to speak about a time without giving it a
character and a name and assuming that anything that happens is
necessarily related to everything that happens. If you think the Nineties
weren't gay, or Hemingway's generation wasn't especially lost, or the
Sixties didn't visibly swing, you have to accept these ideological words
even to argue against them. The same applies to W.H. Auden's dismissal
of the Thirties as 'a low, dishonest decade'. Sociologists posit a spirit of
the age, and then set about documenting it. It can then be endorsed by
whatever supporting evidence the sociologist produces. In theory, the
procedure is harmless. The spirit of an age can be regarded as the ghost in

the machine that exercises power. But it becomes harmful as soon as we imply that the ghost is privileged, and that it should or must be obeyed. At that point it becomes a secular version of God, a personified force which to be obeyed has only to be recognised. In Poland, according to Czeslaw Milosz, 'the successes of Communism among the intellectuals were due mainly to their desire to have value guaranteed, if not by God, at least by history'.*

> *And in Milosz's The Captive Mind: 'Only the blind can fail to see the irony of the situation the human species brought upon itself when it tried to master its own fate and to eliminate accident. It bent its knees to History; and History is a cruel God.'

The harm has been severe in the past few years. It is widely believed that the only thing you can do with the spirit of the age is obey it. Otherwise you convict yourself of being absent from your time and irrelevant to it. But sixty years ago the Modernist writers received as the spirit of the age only the force they set out to defeat. Instead of a spirit of the time officially defined in terms of the march of progress or liberalism or whatever, they wanted to maintain the sense of real time personally or morally charged. True time was kept available by memory, as in Proust, and by a personal or private sense of time, as in Bergson; by certain rarefied moments in Eliot's poetry, and certain historical moments, as in Pound's *Cantos*. Some modern critics have produced a political rhetoric so extreme that if the spirit of the age were as universal as they allege, it would be futile to try to subvert it.

The conceit of a spirit of the age which must be obeyed is far more rampant in the public arts, like architecture, than in the more intimate arts of painting and literature. David Watkin has clarified the matter in his book, *Morality and Architecture*, especially where he discusses, as rhetoricians of architecture, such men as Mies van der Rohe, Le Corbusier, and Sir Nikolaus Pevsner. These theorists agree in specifying a spirit of the age as a collective wisdom working silently, at every moment, towards its fulfilment. There is supposedly a logic of history which should not be resisted. If this were really the case, it would become a moral duty to make it prevail; and indeed these theorists say precisely that. They play down the idea of tradition in favour of such buoyancies as change, progress, development, and revolution. Watkin has pointed out that the rhetoric favours moral relativism 'because of its belief that the spirit has a totally new and homogeneous expression in each epoch, which thereby renders obsolete the cultural, religious, moral, and political patterns of previous epochs.'

It may seem that there is a contradiction between a politics of pluralism and a sociology of the spirit of the age. But there is no contradiction. The conceit of a spirit of the age is quite compatible with pluralism because it offers itself as the wisdom which lies behind every event: it allows room for every attitude, subject to the qualification that history, all the while, is moving towards its fulfilment.

Theorists of the *Zeitgeist* leave the decision to history, but tell you in advance what the decision will be. The politics of pluralism and the sociology of the *Zeitgeist* come together in the high regard we have for change and development. Development is an uplifting notion, it sounds positive, and it provides, as Eliot says in 'The Dry Salvages', 'a means of disowning the past'; it also provides a promise of enhancement for which nobody needs to work, since history is already supposed to be moving toward higher forms of achievement. We identify the good with the future, we make our desires compatible with destiny. If we don't want to exercise judgement, we have the sanction of pluralism for not doing so.

It's a consolation, these days, to be able to identify our motives with the logic of history, because in other respects the social sciences are making gloomy reports. What anthropology mostly offers is remorse. Western societies have allegedly imposed upon primitive people entirely western ways of language, religion, law, and politics. Lévi-Strauss and other anthropologists have interpreted as sinister and domineering every intrusion upon primitive peace. Guilt is the only sentiment we can decently feel. Where anthropology has discovered that we are pre-datory, psychology has discovered that we are fractured. If anthropology and psychology were right, we should thank the god of history for releasing us from the chore of coming to acts of judgement at all.

It follows from the politics of pluralism that the idea of a unified audience has collapsed. The major Modernist writers concerned them-selves with an audience in ways which are no longer available. Yeats and Eliot knew that the question of an audience, in any unified sense, was already acute. Yeats hoped against hope that he might still appeal to a coherent audience by calling it a race and naming the race as Irish. But then he had to admit that the only Irish people he could tolerate were the peasants and aristocrats. So he imagined that the relation between peasant and aristocrat, like the relation between Lady Gregory and her tenants, might be strong enough to suppress the middle class, the small shopkeepers 'fumbling in a greasy till'. Eliot, who agreed with Yeats in little else, agreed with him in despising the middle class. Like other modern writers, he couldn't make up his mind whether he wanted to be read by the few readers likely to understand him or by an ignorant audience which he identified as the lower class.

In his essay on Marie Lloyd he said that the middle class was morally corrupt, and he praised the working class for maintaining a kind of life that could still be expressed in a popular art. 'The working man,' he said, 'who went to the music-hall and saw Marie Lloyd and joined in the chorus was himself performing part of the act; he was engaged in that collaboration of the audience with the artist which is necessary in art and most obviously in dramatic art.' But Eliot's sense of such a collaboration is as archaic as Yeats's. Ken Dodd and Billy Connolly don't address a working-class culture, they are part of a culture defined by middle-class television rather than by the factory or the mine. The pleasure they give their audiences is that of showing that the social system is liberal enough to include them.

Instead of a unified audience, there are hundreds of audiences, groups of people linked by miscellaneous interests. The reason why a distinction between high culture and popular culture is of little use today is that people live by bringing together a collection of disparate images. Some images are held in common by millions of people, but each of us, in turn, diversifies his life by assembling further images, according to procedures of selection impossible to characterise as high or popular. If three hundred million people watch the Eurovision Song Contest, it's mainly for the sense of being one of such a vast number of people looking at the same images for a couple of hours: it can't be with any expectation of hearing songs worth hearing. Television is much concerned with the production of similar images. While it apparently offers a wide choice, the images tend to be the same, like blue jeans. Marshall McLuhan's description of the global village provided by television is true to this extent, that television appeases the common desire to be the same as everybody else. Or at least to have, for a while, the sentiment of being the same. The simultaneous desire to be different is harder to satisfy, but it is satisfied in smaller and more disparate groups.* A cynic might say that the assemblage of images is purely random, and that discrimination isn't involved. But it's more probable that there are several forces at work; caprice, perhaps lethargy, choice, topicality, and various other things. In effect, people make their lives as if they were compiling an anthology.

*'Camp' names such a group; of people who give flamboyantly arbitrary privilege to some few of the proliferating images offered by technology. A principled choice among the

53

Certain items have to be included, or it's not representative enough to be an anthology; but when these items are included, there is space for more informal choices which are thought to be charming if they're not too many or too bizarre. If you live in a city, the range of choice is pretty wide.

images would cancel one's membership of the group. A devotee of Camp disengages appearances from their contexts, and from any loyalties the contexts might propose; then wears the images as style.

Sometimes images are chosen with a high degree of discrimination; sometimes the members are drawn together by the operation of taste, which makes things acceptable. The main characteristic of taste, by extension from its dealing with food and drink, is that it acts immediately without waiting for reasons, it bears the same relation to judgement that an instinct for self-preservation bears to the human body. The difference between discrimination and taste is not that one has reasons and the other hasn't – they both have reasons – it is that one gives reasons and the other doesn't.

In the past few years the politics of pluralism has begun to affect the teaching of literature and the arts in the universities. The traditional view has been that a poem is to be read with such intimacy, concentration, and understanding that the reading issues in an interpretation; the aim is to bring forward the life of the poem, to produce it in the way that a director in the theatre takes a text and gives it life. Teachers presumed to show their students how to do this. Some interpretations were better than others; if a particular reading were wide of the mark, it could be shown to be mistaken. But in the past few years the assumption that one interpretation is more valuable than another has been questioned. The most reasonable form of the question may be found in Frank Kermode's *The Classic*, especially where he points out that a classic, far from insisting upon one reading, is patient of many different ones. *Othello* lives in the different interpretations that readers and theatre directors have offered it. Kermode's attitude is quite reasonable. But it has been taken to wild extremes by those who insist that what matters is each person's experience of the work of art, and that the question of right and wrong doesn't arise. Anything goes.

Pluralism in teaching arose in the Sixties, when students started resenting the official superiority of their teachers. If you were teaching a course in advanced mathematics, you had no challenge of this kind. But if you were teaching a standard course in English or American literature, you could anticipate the claim that every Jack is as good as his master. Stanley Fish and other teachers in American universities found it convenient to concede the claim, and to convince their students by the power of their practice. If Fish gave a remarkably convincing interpretation of one of Milton's poems, he could afford to let every student have his own interpretation, if he wanted it.★ Over the years, some teachers have pushed the political issue further, arguing that schools, colleges, and universities are in league with a domineering society. The authority of a teacher is sometimes compared to that of a judge or a policeman. Some of the challenge is directed at the teacher, some at the authority of what is taught. The idea of a canon in literature and the arts is questioned.§ In many colleges and universities the authority of a canon has broken down; the books to be read are chiefly of symptomatic or sociological interest, and they are read mainly for their bearing upon some social theme, such as violence, sexuality, prejudice, or whatever. It's one of the victories of the social sciences that for certain university courses a television show like *MASH* is more 'relevant' than *King Lear*.

★*As if to say: 'I disagree with your interpretation of "Il Penseroso", but the only thing that matters is your experience in reading the poem.'*

§*No harm in that. The relation between a privileged text and the institution that establishes and maintains it should indeed be questioned.*

It would be wrong to suppose that these matters are mere aberrations to be found in spineless institutions of education. Even in Modernist art and literature, there has long been an antipathy to the exercise of will. André Breton's programme for surrealism involved not only chance and automatism as aesthetic procedures but a cult of passivity, the suspension of the will. The repudiation of will, as if it could be nothing but the will-to-power, has never been far from modern art; the sentiment became more general in the Sixties, especially in America where the will was widely associated with Richard Nixon and American foreign policy. The cult of Oriental postures in philosophy was based upon the idea of releasing oneself from a bad world of politics and power. Stanley Cavell has pointed out that in some modern composers chance is invoked as a principle in much the same way as earlier composers invoked the Muse, to claim that the work of art comes not from the composer but through him. He is the instrument of the Muse, the authority of the work is not his. The difference is that 'speaking for the Muse was to give voice to what all men share, or all would hear; speaking through chance forgoes a voice altogether – there is nothing to say.' But it isn't really content that is hated, rather the will to deliver it.

Jackson Pollock was fully capable of composing a picture, but his drip paintings, such as his 'Cockatoo', are suppressions of the will, leaving everything to chance. The fact that leaving everything to chance is itself an act of will breaks the logic but leaves the paint. The artist presents himself as the medium not of a privileged truth but of whatever happens. And he also exhibits that dissatisfaction with the official conventions of meaning, message, and content which has long been an element in modern art. John Cage's 4'33", in which a pianist sits at a piano, in silence, and raises his hands three times during that period to indicate the end of a movement, is not 4'33" of silence: it's a gesture by which Cage provokes the audience to listen to the casual noises which silence includes, as a more liberal alternative to the formal sequences of an expected music. 'My favourite music,' Cage has said, 'is the one we hear all the time if we are quiet.'

But he has something more in mind. What he repudiates is what I think we have to retain, the convention by which we think of life as a matter of survival, and think of the will as our best means of surviving. Cage often quotes Meister Eckhart's saying that 'we are made perfect by what happens to us rather than by what we do.' Cage repudiates not only the will as a Darwinian insistence on survival but the particular rhythms which he associates with the exercise of will: assertion and denial, crescendo and diminuendo, tension and resolution, which are so much a part of traditional music. 'Boredom dropped when we dropped our interest in climaxes', he has reported. Instead, he would give equal attention to everything.*

This sentiment explains the antagonism aroused by critics who try to discriminate. Think of the gratification most people feel when such a critic has been proved wrong; the French salon-keepers, the critics who rejected the first Impressionist paintings; Nietzsche, Tchaikovsky, Hugo Wolf, and Shaw in their denunciations of Brahms; Walton, who has dismissed Mahler; Ernest Newman, ridiculing Bartok's Violin Sonata. We say that such critics are dogmatic, but we are irritated not by the dogma but by the will exercised in its pronouncement. Our standard reaction is: who does he think he is? But the real reason for discouraging dogma in the criticism of the arts isn't distaste for elitism but the fact that it puts a stop to conversation. Take, for instance, F.R. Leavis's dismissal of Sterne in his study of the English novel, *The*

*Cage's practice as a composer accords with his theory. His String Quartet in Four Parts is charming because it has no audible design upon us, least of all to charm or to affront us. It is enough that it keeps us interested, drawn into a state or mood in which each instrument is accepted as going about its business, paying only enough attention to its companions to ensure the abeyance of tension between them. No wonder one movement is marked 'nearly stationary'.

Great Tradition, where he refers to Sterne's 'irresponsible (and nasty) trifling'. Beyond that phrase, in which even the word 'and' sounds dogmatic, the case against Sterne is not made. What is offensive in the phrase is that Leavis refuses even to discuss the matter: he refuses, by more than implication, the company of anyone who would want to.

Lionel Trilling offered to discuss it, while first accepting the strong emphasis that Leavis put upon the importance of 'marked moral intensity'; just as Trilling accepted that 'it is upon the degree and quality of moral intensity that all aesthetic considerations of the novel depend.' But he argued that Leavis didn't take any proper account of 'the art that delights — and enlightens — by the intentional relaxation of moral awareness, by its invitation to us to contemplate the mere excess of irrelevant life.' Clearly, there is the making of a genuine argument in Trilling's response; but Leavis didn't deign to notice that an offer to debate the question had even been made. If such a situation occurred in the sciences; if a scientist didn't even consider taking up a colleague's rival argument; it would be regarded as disgraceful. But in the arts there is no convention by which the decencies of debate are observed.

The matter of debate becomes much more tendentious where boundaries of expertise are crossed. Would an art critic take up an argument started by someone who is not by profession an art critic? I'm thinking of such things as Foucault's essay on the 'Las Meninas' of Velasquez; Gilles Deleuze's book on Francis Bacon's paintings; Julia Kristeva's essay on Giotto's frescoes for the Arena Chapel in Padua. I doubt if any of these has been given a place in the professional study of its subject.* It may be, of course, that the habit of pluralism has entered so fully into criticism of the arts that a critical debate rarely arises. Let anyone say whatever he wants to say, subject to the reservation that nothing said will be taken seriously enough to be questioned. But there may be a more acceptable explanation. None of the essays I have mentioned is a disinterested account of its subject: each is for the sake of something else, an argument on a larger theme for which the essay on a painting is merely an illustration. The larger theme is not an aesthetic question: it's sometimes philosophical but more often political. Indeed, one of the clearest marks of contemporary criticism of the arts is that, when it entails judgements, the judgements

*Not quite true. 'Las Meninas' has provoked a running argument between Foucault, the philosopher John Searle, and the art critic Leo Steinberg. Van Gogh's 'Vieux souliers aux lacets' has been an issue between Heidegger, Jacques Derrida, and the art historian Meyer Schapiro. Admirable exceptions, these.

are political rather than aesthetic.

There is a well-known essay by Roland Barthes called 'The Grain of the Voice'. Basically, it's about the singer Dietrich Fischer-Dieskau, whose singing Barthes didn't like. He acknowledged his talent, but he remained hostile to his style. Barthes maintained that Fischer-Dieskau's singing is perfect, but that it is a perfection that answers the demands of an average culture. The culture is petit-bourgeois, it wants its music to be expressive, to translate 'emotion' into communicative forms. In Fischer-Dieskau's singing the diction is dramatic, the pauses, the checkings and releases of breath occur like shudders of passion. His art is totally devoted to the soul, as distinct from the body; to the breath, separated from the muscles, the stubborn weight; it's devoted to expression as distinct from significance. The breath in such singing is felt as the soul's swelling or breaking; it's a mystical art, denying the body in its aspiration toward purity. 'With Fischer-Dieskau,' Barthes says, 'I seem only to hear the lungs, never the tongue, the glottis, the teeth, the mucous membrane, the nose.' And he contrasts him with Panzera, a singer we don't know very well because he sang before the age of the LP. 'You never heard him breathe,' Barthes says, 'but only dividing up the phrase.' Not the breath of lungs, but the letters, the syllables of a language. Barthes disapproves of any art that merely makes itself available to gratify its culture.

According to this view, Fischer-Dieskau is flattering petit-bourgeois society by offering it an image of its own perfection, of the sense of itself as perfect. He allows his talent to coincide with the particular kind of perfection a petit-bourgeois culture dreams of. Panzera's art, apparently, set itself aslant its culture. For the same reason, Barthes prefers Landowska to other harpsichordists, and Lipatti to other pianists: their playing is never flattened into perfection, they don't add an intention to the music or fuss over its every detail, contrary to petit-bourgeois art which, according to Barthes, is 'always indiscreet'.

Barthes's essay on Fischer-Dieskau depends upon politics rather than aesthetics. He has no time for a perception that doesn't take sides. Where Trilling argued that 'it is upon the degree and quality of moral intensity that all aesthetic considerations of the novel depend', Barthes argued that every aesthetic merit depends upon an interrogative and ultimately subversive relation between the art and its society. There should always be a certain recalcitrance. The trouble with Barthes's position was that it had conditions attached: he had a particular idea of society in view and indeed a particular axe to grind. He merely answered one ideology with a manifesto for another. But art is not just hostile to our particular form of society; it is neither left wing nor right wing. It's antagonistic not to reality but to any and every official knowledge of it. This antagonism should be maintained whether the official determination of society is bourgeois liberal, Marxist, aristocratic or Fascist. That's why aesthetics must never degenerate into politics or psychology. Both are reductive and play into the hands of a society which likes nothing better than to reduce the arts to the form of knowledge it already enforces.

Commentary

This one didn't irritate its listeners, apparently. It may not have interested them.

On the question of chance, randomness, and the suspension of the will; I might have mentioned James Merrill's ouija-board poems, which seem to me arch and, for that reason, much inferior to the poems in which he exercises the avowed power of his judgement. But the theoretical issues involved in chance and randomness are very difficult. The physicist Werner Brandt once offered to guide me through Jacques Monod's *Chance and Necessity*, but I let the invitation lapse.

I should have pressed harder on the question of aesthetic judgement. Is an aesthetic judgement possible which is not the result of prior judgements in, perhaps, ethics or politics? In 1935 Eliot put forward the proposition that 'literary criticism should be completed by criticism from a definite ethical and theological standpoint.' But this proposition doesn't answer my question; it merely says that a criticism which doesn't take a definite ethical and theological position is incomplete.

Early in the lecture, I find, the words 'pluralist' and 'play' occur in the same sentence. I don't recall any special consideration in lodging them there. But it now strikes me that 'play', at least in the particular sense in which Jacques Derrida uses the word *le jeu*, play or freeplay, could be regarded as the personal form of pluralism; pluralism brought to bear upon one's own intellectual acts and declared in one's favour. I want to develop this notion a good deal further, starting with the fact that pluralism involves the acknowledgement, with whatever goodwill, of more than one ultimate principle. It can arise from various considerations. A society might consider itself strong enough in its ideology to accommodate any number of minor interests and values; as a strong government welcomes opposition parties so that local sentiments of envy, fear, or rage may be vented without having to be carried into action in the streets. Or a society might feel that its authority depends not upon ideological strength but upon a low-level coalition of interests, none of which is strong enough to serve as the basis of government. The parliamentary form of this pluralism is a system of small parties and shifting alliances: no voice can safely be suppressed because you might need it at any time to keep you and your friends in office. A government by coalition always represents as essential what keeps its several parties together, and as inessential the values which divide them. But in any case it has to allow for considerable diversity. As for people: most people want strong governments to act as if they were weak, and weak governments to act as if they were strong: the first case shows that the governors are not only strong, but decent, the second that they are not so weak as to lack courage and resolution.

It follows from pluralism that the virtue people are supposed to acquire is tolerance. In the arts, intolerance of anything is considered a mortal sin; that is, a naïveté. The reason why the avant-garde motive persists in music more than in any other art is that tolerance in the ear is far harder than in the eye. There are physiological reasons for the fact that dissonance is more painful to hear than hideous visual images are to see. It is easier, too, to shut your eyes or turn away than to stop your ears: pressing your earlobes is not efficient. Tolerance is also suggested by whatever we have learnt to accept not only in satire but in parody, the spoof, burlesque, the hoax, unstable irony in which the ostensible ground of the first irony is itself undermined; also in black humour, the exigencies of open form, and the put-on, the last of these being what Jacob Brackman has described in terms of our 'fascination with the possibly fraudulent'. Many of these can be understood by thinking of disparate audiences and then of someone who, crossing from one audience to another, pretends not to know that he has done so. At a party someone comes up to you and introduces himself as an undercover agent for the Green Berets. Your silent reaction is one of these: he is; he isn't, he's lying; he's pretending, mainly to see whether I can spot the pretence; he's joking; maybe he's not joking. The put-on is made possible by the diversity of groups, the exotic possibility of entering an alien group as a stranger, and the tolerance now obligatory as a mark of being liberal.

But a further step brings me to the second word. If you were to take pluralism seriously and give yourself the benefit of it, you would engage in play. Not in role-playing, merely: because there the roles are set out in advance (husband, breadwinner, Democrat, and so on) and you play the roles according to criteria and procedures not of your own making. In play, you don't accept any rules or conventions, except the first one, of affronting the official ones. Play is the pluralism you take to yourself, normally as a release from the burden of your several duties.

In Nietzsche, the idea of play is sometimes turned toward the chance and necessity of gambling, the throw of the dice, as in *Thus Spoke Zarathustra*, especially the chapter 'Of the Higher Man'. Or, in the same place, it is linked to the dance, in keeping with Nietzsche's grounding of art in the life of the human body, according to a physiological aesthetic. In *The Will to Power* Nietzsche proposes the image of the child at play as the supreme image, beyond all conflicts of good and evil: 'Play, the useless – as the ideal of him who is overfull of strength, as "childlike".' The uselessness of art is its finest attribute, because it does not take part in the rigmarole of purposes and ends. A typical gesture in *The Birth of Tragedy* is: 'Only as an aesthetic phenomenon are the world and the existence of man eternally justified.' In *The Will to Power*: 'We possess art lest we perish of the Truth.' In these gestures Nietzsche wants to circumvent the privilege of morality and truth by locating the value of an action in its unintentional character; or rather, in its refusal of an intention. And in *The Gay Science* the chosen act is that of improvisation in music, where the musician plays without an object or a goal, turning even his mistakes into opportunities for new directions. Beyond good and evil: that is, beyond the question of moral choice, official values, the privileging of fellowship and selflessness.

The common factor in these motifs is the transfer to the subject, the agent, of the causes conventionally found in nature. One should not, Nietzsche says in *Beyond Good and Evil*, make 'cause' and 'effect' into material things or make cause press and push till it 'produces an effect'. One should employ 'cause' and 'effect' only as pure concepts, conventional fictions for the purpose of designation, not explanation. 'It is we alone who have fabricated causes, succession, reciprocity, relativity, compulsion, number, law, freedom, motive, purpose.' It is mere mythology to introduce these symbols into things as though symbols were found in nature; they are conceived in men. Existence has no meaning except whatever meaning we give it. In the same spirit, as Heidegger pointed out, Nietzsche insisted that the old aesthetic was always an aesthetic of passive, receptive consumers: we must make it one of producers, in another act of transference. Regrettably, though inevitably, Nietzsche associated this distinction with one between man and woman. 'Our aesthetic was a feminine one in that only those natures which were receptive to art formulated their experience of "what is beautiful".' The artist, whom Nietzsche regards as masculine, has been lacking: there has only been an aesthete, a philosopher of art, responsive, accepting, a mere woman.

These Nietzschean themes have been forwarded by Jacques Derrida in his book on Nietzsche's styles, *Éperons*, but it is clear that they have long participated in a celebrated distinction Derrida proposed between two kinds of interpretation; though he stopped well short of Nietzsche's offensive denomination of man and woman. Derrida distinguished two interpretations of interpretation, but it would have been better if he had called one interpretation and the other play. In *L'écriture et le différence* he posited, in any case, two kinds of interpretation. The first is the ordinary one. We read a text, trying to understand it. We look for its structure, and assume that the structure is stabilised by its centre, a point of presence, a fixed origin. The centre would permit the play of the elements of the work, but only within the total form: the centre opens up play and closes it off. 'The concept of centred structure is the concept of a play based on a fundamental ground, a play constituted on the basis of a fundamental immobility and a reassuring certitude, which itself is beyond the reach of play.' The gratification of finding such a centre is that anxiety is allayed, the anxiety that arises from 'being caught in a game' or 'from being at stake in the game'. This form of interpretation is based upon 'the determination of Being as presence in all senses of that word'. It is also based upon an assumed relation between the sign and that of which it is the sign; between signifier and signified. Interpretation, in this sense, is an attempt to discover and acknowledge the work in its meaning.

A second kind of interpretation is what we call play. It assumes that the text is without a centre, the structure is without a centre: the centre is not to be found, but it may be thought not as a fixed locus but as a function, 'a sort of non-locus in which an infinite number of sign-substitutions come into play.' Precisely because of the absence of the transcendental signified, the play of signification is extended indefinitely. Since there is no centre which would arrest the play of substitutions, the play supplements the lack: in the absence of a signified, the sign is a surplus of signification. The lack is made up for by the abundance of the signifier.

Derrida goes on to say that play disrupts presence. 'Play is always play of absence and presence, but if it is to be radically conceived, it must be conceived before the alternative of presence and absence. Being must be conceived as presence or absence on the basis of the possibility of play and not the other way round.' For a similar reason, play breaks the complicity of presence and history, since history has always been conceived of as a detour between two presences. Finally:

63

There are thus two interpretations of interpretation, of structure, of sign, of play. The one seeks to decipher, dreams of deciphering a truth or an origin which escapes play and the order of the sign and which lives the necessity of interpretation as an exile. The other, which is no longer turned toward the origin, affirms play and tries to pass beyond man and humanism, the name of man being the name of that being who, throughout the history of metaphysics or of ontotheology – in other words, throughout his entire history – has dreamed of full presence, the reassuring foundation, the origin and the end of play.

Derrida's main authority for play is, of course, Nietzsche, 'the Nietzschean affirmation, that is the joyous affirmation of the play of the world and of the innocence of becoming, the affirmation of a world of signs without fault, without truth, and without origin which is offered to an active interpretation.' This affirmation 'then determines the noncentre otherwise than as loss of the centre'; and it plays without security.

Between interpretation and play, according to Derrida, there is no choice, because 'we are in a region – let's say, provisionally, a region of historicity – where the category of choice seems particularly trivial.' But he points not toward choice but toward a vision, which naturally seems a monstrous birth, as if he were saying, with Yeats, 'After us the Savage God.' Or, again with Yeats, as if he were glossing Nietzsche's tragic joy, laughter in the face of death. Still with Yeats, a title for Derrida's work: *Where There is Nothing*.

What does Derrida's distinction between interpretation and play amount to? It accords with Nietzsche's distinction between responsive, receptive woman and productive man; between consumer and producer. Interpretation takes up the hermeneutic project and postulates a true sense of the text: it acts within 'the horizon of the meaning or truth of being', the values of 'the product's production and the present's presence'. In play, on the other hand, meaning is a function of play, 'inscribed in a certain place in the configuration of a meaningless play'.

The clearest account of play, not in its practice but as its practice might come about, is Derrida's essay on Artaud and the Theatre of Cruelty in *L'écriture et la différence*. I shall give the gist of the argument, not pausing to indicate precisely where Derrida begins or Artaud ends. The basic point is that the conventional theatre of the West has always been a dialogue between theology and humanism; between the word and man as the beneficiary of its meaning. This dialogue would be broken in the Theatre of Cruelty, which would reduce the privilege of words and refuse to deal in a theatre which merely illustrates a prior discourse. The Theatre of Cruelty repudiates form in favour of force; repudiates imitation or representation, or anything that implies that the truth is elsewhere and is now to be translated into representative words. Conventional theatre, dominated by speech, is equally slavish toward the author, the printed or printable text, and the passive, seated audience. Instead, the Theatre of Cruelty will proclaim the *mise en scène*, 'spectacle acting not as reflection but as force': it will respect of words not their logical and discursive intentions, their rational transparency, but their primordial resonance. Derrida refers to 'the shout that the articulations of language and logic have not yet entirely frozen, the aspect of oppressed gesture which remains in all speech, the unique and irreplaceable movement which the generalities of concept and repetition have never finished rejecting.' The Theatre of Cruelty 'is less a question of constructing a mute stage than of constructing a stage whose clamor has not yet been pacified into words'. It will utter 'the speech before words'. In that capacity, it engages not with what already exists but with the imaginary which, not yet existent, tries to exist. But its particular mark is that it rejects the conceptual or symbolic closure imposed by discourse.

If my version of the field of force in Nietzsche, Artaud, and Derrida is accurate, it would seem that I should endorse it without reservation. Isn't it an attempt to force liberal humanists to acknowledge what they have long hated to acknowledge, the primordial cry, the unpacified gesture? Where is mystery to be sensed if not 'beyond good and evil'? Even if the Theatre of Cruelty has already been domesticated, recited as a chapter in the history of the theatre, shouldn't I endorse its force? But my reservation is such that it amounts to a rejection. Derrida wants to retain of words nothing but their primordial gesture: he regards as so much dross the discursive commitment of words. He is a Manichee, not merely a Nietzschean; for him, the bourgeois domain of good and evil is enforced by language in its logical, discursive, semantic character. Play is what is left; it corresponds to the primordial cry, the speech before the fall into words and the sin of grammar. He wants the resonance of words without the words; or without their bourgeois piety. But the resonance is empty, and the desire for it is sentimental.

It is a sentimentality, and not only an error of judgement, to divide words into (a) their discursive duty and (b) the oppressed or aboriginal

65

gesture which bourgeois duty has nearly suppressed. Desdemona says to Othello: 'I understand a fury in your words, but not the words.' It is for the sake of an empty resonance that one would sense the fury in the words and throw away the rest. In *Glas* and *Éperons* what Derrida values is not words as they try to mean or to mean more, but the punning eventfulness they make possible; as if he wanted to defeat the dutiful intentions of words by pointing up their arbitrary, ephemeral qualities, the coincidence of letters and syllables. But the only resonance worth attending to is what issues from words as they try to reach beyond or beneath their discursive properties. 'Language as gesture' is most fully realised not when its speaking intention is discarded but when it speaks with a sense of its own limits. 'The language of silence' speaks of its limits. I want to feel the fury in the words as a quality of words in the way they are, which includes – with whatever degree of failure – the way they mean.

I started with the proposition that play is one's own pluralism, a release from the orthodoxy of discourse. Derrida is my example. Many of his pages, especially in *Glas*, deal with words as if the sins of grammar and syntax had not yet been committed; as if it were still possible to forestall the catastrophe. On the other hand he has written hundreds of pages as orthodox as anyone else's, lucid in themselves if not a cause of lucidity in his pupils. No vision of play 'beyond good and evil' has enabled him to evade discourse: his work, despite the punning, is discursive through and through. The real scandal, from a Derridean point of view, is that discourse has been able to accommodate his writing.

But there is another tradition by which 'play' may be understood and pointed toward a different end. A full account of that tradition would involve an elaborate commentary on certain principles in Kant, Schiller, Gadamer, Winnicott, and Marcuse; an odd assortment, you may protest, but companionable in the present context. From Schiller's *Letters on the Aesthetic Education of Man* to Marcuse's *The Aesthetic Dimension* and Gadamer's *Truth and Method*, there is one emphasis from which a theory of artistic production might be deduced; it is the association of artistic production with freedom, and it issues in the association of that freedom with play; the 'impulse of play', which Schiller calls *Spiel-trieb*. I want to make sure not to confound these texts or to blur their differences: it will be enough if I suggest the paradigm of artistic production which would find authority, allowing for degrees of emphasis, in each of them.

66

The most thoroughgoing assertion of play in relation to freedom comes in Schiller's fifteenth letter, where he claims that 'Man plays only when he is in the full sense of the word a human being, and he is a perfect human being only when he plays.' It is through the experience of beauty, Schiller argues, that one reaches the experience of freedom. The reason is that in every other activity one is under some degree of constraint. Just as a work of art is such to the degree to which it appears to be as spontaneous as nature; so, in the aesthetic experience, the operative laws of existence are made compatible with the terms of the individual will. Beauty, according to Schiller, is 'freedom in appearance'; a work of art is determined neither by the material of which it is made nor by any purpose it may be made to serve – whether that purpose is practical, intellectual, or moral. So it is necessary to distinguish between moral freedom and aesthetic freedom. Moral freedom is the freedom to choose to act in one way rather than another: aesthetic freedom is the freedom to postpone all such choices, and to remain in the enjoyment of one's general capacity. 'When we remember', Schiller says, 'that it is precisely this freedom which is withheld from man by the one-sided constraint which nature imposes on his feelings, and by the exclusive legislation of reason in his thinking, we must regard the capacity which is restored to him in the aesthetic mood as the highest of all gifts, the gift of humanity itself.'

Schiller wrote the *Letters* in 1795. Within fifty years, society had determined that reality would be taken as an established fact, established in terms of the exchange of goods, technology, the privileging of scientific criteria. Inevitably, the play-impulse was set aside as trivial, any and every way of consuming vacant time; leisure-activities. The distinction between accredited work and trivial leisure had the effect of relegating the arts as superior amusements. It would be a wild conceit, at this stage, to imagine that the nineteenth century would have taken a different direction: but it might have derived a politics and a morality from an aesthetics. It might have retained Schiller's sense of the correlation of humanity, freedom, play, and aesthetic experience; even if it had gone on to pursue, as second-best purposes, the aims it did in fact pursue as the only purposes that counted.

In the event, as we know and as I mentioned in my first lecture, the nineteenth century defined its aims in terms which dismissed the serious artist and forced him to prescribe, in varying degrees of resentment and desperation, a rival world of forms and cadences which had every merit except accredited existence in the world. In turn, the definition of reality in terms which, if articulated and named, would amount to logical positivism in one form or another had the effect of dividing experience into two characters; an official one, deemed to be verifiable by scientific methods and therefore authentic; and everything else, the suspect residue, which could hardly be denied in fact but could be ascribed to impulse wilful, deluded, childish, fantastic, or otherwise vacuous. A corresponding division was prescribed in language: what we call discourse was prescribed as the language appropriate to reality, verified now by the syntax of commonsense and communication: every other form of language was deemed to be poetic, demotic, occult in one degree or another.

It is in this context that *The Aesthetic Dimension* is important. Marcuse's Marxist credentials are such that he can't be written off as a mere poet. But here he is, on the first page of the book, asserting that 'by virtue of its aesthetic form, art is largely autonomous vis à vis the given social relations.' The political potential of art, he continues, lies only in its own aesthetic dimension:

> The radical qualities of art, that is to say, its indictment of the
> established reality and its invocation of the beautiful image (*schöner
> Schein*) of liberation are grounded precisely in the dimensions where
> art *transcends* its social determination and emancipates itself from
> the given universe of discourse and behaviour while preserving its
> overwhelming presence. Thereby art creates the realm in which
> the subversion of experience proper to art becomes possible: the
> world formed by art is recognised as a reality which is suppressed
> and distorted in the given reality.

It follows that 'the truth of art lies in its power to break the monopoly of established reality (i.e. of those who established it) to *define* what is *real*.' And that art 'is committed to that perception of the world which alienates individuals from their functional existence and performance in society – but this achievement presupposes a degree of autonomy which withdraws art from the mystifying power of the given and frees it for the expression of its own truth.'

Marcuse speaks of freedom, not of play. But the connexion is easily made. What else is play but the exercise of freedom as, in Schiller's terms, a general capacity? Of course Marcuse is a man of his time, he accepts that in practice the world is as it has become; he values art, as I do, for its

THE PARADE OF IDEAS

power of contradiction, its protest against a narrow definition of reality and the prescription of its forms. It is too late to think of going back to 1795. But it may still be possible to speak up for the general human capacity, which Schiller represents as freedom exercised in play, and to locate it, in the human narrative, prior to any of the local interests we refer to as roles and functions. Newman's idea of a university might be invoked as the scene in which a general human capacity is acknowledged and furthered, distinct from any of the particular roles which are furthered in the professional schools of medicine, engineering, and so forth.

But we are ignoring the context in which play and freedom are exercised. What is the clearest and truest thing we can say about the arts in modern societies? Answer: that they offer to one's attention millions of images, their proliferation such that nobody could respond to them in ten lifetimes. The one clear thing is: they are too many. We have our historical sense to thank for the proliferation. Or rather, our grand-fathers. André Malraux has claimed, in *The Voices of Silence*, that the crucial historical event of the nineteenth century was the birth of a new consciousness of history. But nineteenth-century artists, newly alerted to history, had only a tolerable amount of it to be alerted to. The privilege of Greek culture in nineteenth-century Europe arose from the fact that the remnants of Greece, in sculpture, literature, and philosophy, were at hand: you could read the epics, see the statues, steal the Elgin Marbles. The remnants of other cultures were relatively invisible. Even fifty years ago, it was still possible to say what the official texts of culture were. I find it remarkable, none the less, that Eliot, writing in 1919, described the historical sense as compelling a man to write 'not merely with his own generation in his bones, but with a feeling that the whole of the literature of Europe from Homer and within it the whole of the literature of his own country has a simultaneous existence and composes a simultaneous order'. Eliot's order was a tall one in 1919, and it has become outlandish, now that anthropologists have schooled us to give up thinking of Europe as if it were the universe. We are now required to be equally attentive to the remnants of historical life in every continent, or stand convicted of parochialism. No text is more official than any other: if you think that Greek civilisation is more valuable than Mayan, you have to justify the thought. I agree with Geoffrey Hartman when he writes, in *The Fate of Reading*, that 'the growth of the historical consciousness, its multiplying of disparate models all of which press their claim, amounts to a peculiarly modern burden.' To be aware of the past, Hartman says, 'is to be surrounded by abstract potentialities, imperatives that cannot all be heeded, options exhausting the power of choice'.

It follows that the simultaneous order which Eliot invoked is a dream of order, and nothing more. The proliferation of images from every known society can be felt as plenitude, but not as order: apart from many other considerations, these images have had to lose their historical significance so as to gain the boon of ending in our museums. Our relation to them is synchronic, not diachronic. The work of culture in the age of mechanical reproduction, to revert to Walter Benjamin's theme, loses its historical density by becoming picturesque; we welcome it as a picture and not as an action or a narrative. Indeed, the notion of play, and – I would now want to add – the even more fashionable notion of indeterminacy in interpretation, are attractive to us, I think, as a strategic answer to the surfeit of cultural images calling for attention. It is inevitable that we devise several strategies for neutralising the claims a cultural image makes. The proliferation of claims delivered with these images would be intolerable if we couldn't devise ways of neutralising them. Indifference is a help, but it is not decent. Indeterminacy is an answer to proliferation; so is play; and so is the habit of voiding claims upon our attention by declaring them all equally arbitrary. These procedures are feasible because there is no longer a Greek or Roman authority; no *imperium*. We are free as we move about our imaginary museum. When all else is at risk of failing, we can always reduce the claims of history by declaring history a fiction like any other.

These considerations might well have preoccupied my next lecture, but they didn't; my context turned out to be much narrower.

FOUR

THE CHERISHING BUREAUCRACY

If you wanted to neutralise the arts and remove their mystery, the best strategy would be to reduce them to psychology and politics, and then apply to them the secular techniques of management, to show that they are at least in that respect like any other activity.* This is exactly what has happened. But I shouldn't make it sound too sinister. Michel Foucault and other critics have interpreted this sentiment as in every way reprehensible: they see in modern societies a determination to constrain every human impulse, and they allege that the most typical institutions of society are the law-courts, the prisons, insane asylums, and bureaucracy, rather than the Red Cross. I prefer to think that modern societies insist on understanding every impulse, if necessary by procedures extremely reductive, but they are not obsessed by images of constraint. Foucault's argument is too global to be convincing.§ But I have to concede that modern societies have a surprising interest in assimilating the arts; you would have thought that the arts could safely be allowed to go their own way. In a sense, of course, they are. But saying this reminds me of the anger young people in the Sixties felt toward 'benevolent paternalism'. Fathers were kind, warm-hearted, generous enough to subsidise a social revolution, but their motives were suspect; they were especially tender in the hope that their children would not strike them. The question is: do modern societies domesticate the arts because they can't bear not to comprehend them, or because they are determined to keep everything under control? Foucault goes for the extreme answer; I want to keep the question open.

*The arts, because they can be enjoyed only at leisure, give us the feeling of being released from the routines of a consuming society. We live, for the time being, according to different moods and rhythms. This is the easiest, and not the weakest, argument for the arts.

§Frank Lentricchia has argued, most persuasively, that in Foucault's social theory power tends to occupy the 'anonymous' place which classical treatises in metaphysics reserved for substance: without location, identity, or boundaries, it is everywhere and nowhere at the same time. 'Because he leaves no shaded zone, no free space for real alternatives to take form, Foucault's vision of power, despite its provisions for reversals of direction, courts a monolithic determinism . . .

I've stressed the reductive motive, thinking especially of psychology and politics, but there's one part of
psychoanalytical theory which supports my argument
that the typical social act is the elimination of mystery
by reducing reality to forms in which it may be
administered. It is Jacques Lacan's distinction between
desire and need. What corresponds in the human
psyche to mystery in the arts is what he calls desire,
which is desire only because it is unconscious and

*there is no alternative space
out of which he can propel the
changes implied by his accu-
sation. His theory of discipline
cannot explain why he himself
is not a mindless zombie, how
he himself can mount a criticism of the system.'*

ineffable. What he calls need is a drive that can be met, like hunger or
thirst. It is a specific detail of compulsion; your body would protest if you
didn't satisfy it. But desire is lack, it can't be met, because it is
categorical and therefore endless. It is the condition of life as such, not a
particular craving which can be satisfied. The distinction corresponds to
the one between mystery and problem. The management of the arts
is a system by which it is pretended that desire is the same as need and
may be appeased by money and fame. If it were successful, it would complete the secularisation of their spirituality, a process well established
in the universities, where the most radical arts are taught, defined and
assimilated.

Some years ago, Lionel Trilling taught the course in modern literature
at Columbia College, choosing major works by Yeats, Eliot, Joyce,
Proust, Kafka, Lawrence, Mann, and Conrad, works which meant much
to him because of the questions they propose for one's moral life. But he
found that teaching these works had the effect of calming them, drawing
them into a process of recognition and acceptance. He found, too, that
students were quite willing to take part in this process: they looked into
the abyss opened up by Conrad's *Heart of Darkness* and came back
undaunted. By the time these great works had been put through the
routines of discussion, commentary, examination papers and grades, they
had lost their power to hurt, and their power to
sustain had become mechanical.*

The administration of the arts begins with the
moment in which we give them their names. As soon
as you think of something as a sculpture, you have a
slot for it: it's because the word 'sculpture' is available
that we can talk about it. The object may challenge
these considerations or refute them, but at least they
are there. The next stage in management is the assign-

*In The Notebooks of
Malte Laurids Brigge
Rilke, thinking of Ibsen, says:
'Loneliest of men, holding
aloof from them all, how
quickly they have caught up
with you because of your
fame. A little while ago they*

ment of a place. Certain works of art are given a place in public recognition, certain buildings are set aside for them: galleries, concert halls, in London the South Bank as an artistic ghetto. These are special places, secular temples; when you enter, you lower your voice. And bureaucracy determines not just what will be seen but how it will be seen. A sculpture exhibited in a gallery offers a certain experience: if it were in a shopping centre or a field, it would raise questions about art and nature which an art gallery doesn't raise. In a gallery, everything is already culture. While you're there, you don't think about art and nature, or whether the diverse claims of each have been concili- ated, you don't even think about art as an enhancement

were against you body and soul; and now they treat you as their equal. And they pull your words around with them in the cages of their presumption, and exhibit them in the streets, and tease them a little, from a safe distance. All your terrifying wild beasts.' Modern societies pacify their artists, and buy them off, by giving them fame.

of your environment. A gallery is not the best place to look at paintings, precisely because it is the best place to study the history of art; for the same reason that people become interested in 'comparative religion' when they have given up believing in any of the religions they compare.

Works of art come into galleries and concert halls sometimes by one man's decision but more often by official patronage. Patronage is the Berenson of our time, and its commonest name is the Arts Council or Mobil Oil or words to that effect. These days it tends to come from a committee or a network of advisory committees. I don't automatically assume, by the way, that a decision taken by a committee is wrong and that one taken by an individual is right. Institutions have had a bad press. Critics who have written about academies, whether Russian, French, or British, or whatever, have maintained that such institutions are the instruments of official power; that they are designed, as John Berger says, 'to ensure the continuation of a traditional, homogeneous art reflecting the State ideology', whether that ideology is conservative or progressive. The Academy, he says, 'centralises all artistic activity and regularises all standards and judgements . . . and the rules, instead of being deduced from particular examples or models at hand, are now induced as abstractions which schematise and inhibit the artist's imagi- nation before he even begins to work.'

Now I'm sure some academics have done precisely that. When Sir Joshua Reynolds, Benjamin West, Gainsborough and other artists per- suaded King George III to establish the Royal Academy in 1768, they had an interest in stabilising art by prescribing its rules. 'Every opportunity should be taken', Reynolds said, 'to discountenance the false and vulgar opinion that rules are the fetters of genius. They are fetters only to men of no genius; as that armour, which upon the strong is an ornament, cripples the body which it was made to protect.' But the situation has changed in ways which may not be an improvement. I don't believe that modern academies are trying to maintain a traditional, homogeneous art reflecting the State ideology. The only serious, documented attack on the Arts Council in this matter, during the past few years, so far as its dealing with painting is an issue, has accused the Council of favouring one school of art: minimal, post-constructivist abstraction. It has been argued that the same few artists keep coming up as prize-winners, the same few galleries are given something like official acknowledgement, and that the Council has largely ignored good artists who work in realist or figurative styles.* Now it might be possible to see some connection between minimal, post-constructivist abstraction and the governments in office during the past several years, but I doubt it.

It is more probable that in a pluralist ethos a slight push in one direction rather than another is enough to set things moving. It's hard to believe that there are strong ideological forces at work which issue in the promotion of Victor Burgin or Stuart Brizley. I deduce from the evidence not the lesson that John Berger has drawn in such ominous terms, but the far more serious conclusion, that the State isn't interested in any style, and that, if it has to choose one, it settles readily enough for the most avant-garde style it can find, subject to a time-lag of a couple of years. What the State seems to be saying is: artists can do whatever they like, because nothing they do makes any difference to anyone. The advantage of choosing an avant-garde style of some kind is that the State can't then be accused of enforcing a traditional style in keeping with its ideology. The ICA or the Hayward Annual is just as acceptable to the State as the Royal Academy's Summer Show, because none of them makes any difference.

*Richard Hoggart has recently argued in a BBC radio discussion, with an evident intention of refuting my position, that the grants and awards given by the Arts Council are decided, in practice, by several committees. The Council sets up these committees; but, once established, each acts like a branch of the Mafia, with spheres of influence, territories, and the like. But this argument doesn't disturb my claim that the Council isn't concerned with critical discrimination: the aims of the Council are administrative, managerial, and – in those contexts – rhetorical.

Once the arts become visible, and works of art become public events in this way, they also become commodities. Leo Castelli's dealing in Pop Art may be understood by comparing it with anyone's dealing in a new product: he surmounted the same problems of production, advertising, sales, taxation, and so on. There is no reason to think that the pleasure of his dealing with the paintings excluded aesthetic satisfaction. The fact that the products then entered the system of exhibitions, reviews, gossip, sales, colour reproductions, and celebrity arises without further ado from the general culture of commodities.

Of course this isn't a recent development; it would be naive to think that the motives of the eighteenth-century Grub Street were purer than those to be discovered in the galleries of Madison Avenue. There is no point in warming ourselves with a pastoral vision, based upon nostalgia for agricultural communities and the charm of a wheelwright engaged in his craft. But the modern situation has two characteristics which are particularly important to the technique of management. The first is that the product can hardly be said to exist, till a name has been found for it. To call it 'art' is merely to start the process. And the second is that the quality of the work of art is, in practical terms, a secondary issue.

I've referred to Pop Art. Before it got its name, certain paintings were invisible in the sense that those who looked at them couldn't see them as anything in particular or, more to the point, as any class of thing more specific than the large class of being paintings. The name made the paintings visible by making them discussable: you could talk about them without standing in front of one. The same applies to every school or movement in the arts. In 1952 when Harold Rosenberg wrote an essay called 'The American Action Painters,' he achieved several aims at the same time. He brought certain paintings together. He clarified, even for the artists themselves, what they were doing, and why. He surrounded those paintings with a discourse so congenial to them that it has been impossible, ever since, to separate them from his programme. It's still a question whether the discourse arose from the paintings, or went beyond them in a direction they merely indicated. But in any case the discourse set the terms in which the paintings continue to be seen: 'the canvas is an arena in which to act': 'what was to go on the canvas was not a picture but an event': action painting 'offers its hand to pantomime and dance': 'action painting is painting in the medium of difficulties.' These are the terms in which the paintings are seen. Now it would be wrong to say that Rosenberg not only made them visible but told people what to think about them. He permitted people to think of them by giving them the words in which they could discuss them. The name 'Action Painting' is like a table of contents, it indicates the terms of the discussion to follow.

It could be argued in a cynical spirit that Rosenberg's naming of Action Painting, useful as it was, was itself a managerial act; that it moved certain paintings into the auction rooms and stuck a label on them, increasing their price without altering their value. Now that's true; but what I admire in his essay is the delicacy with which he took care not to imply that the paintings were fully explained by the name or exhausted by the description he provided. The word 'action' made the paintings seem serious, which they are, and the fact that the concept of action is virtually inexhaustible in modern philosophy made a space for them in relation to a continuing argument.

But there is a problem in such lucidity. The phrases which have been devised to make the arts comprehensible are rarely innocent, they often make larger claims than the works themselves justify. The callow notion that life is absurd has certainly been promoted by the label 'Absurdist Drama' affixed to a few unremarkable plays. The name 'Minimal Art' carries a suggestion of self-denial and asceticism not endorsed by Tony Smith and his colleagues in the works themselves. The problem with such phrases is that they don't so much describe any particular paintings or sculptures as the category they are supposed to inhabit: once the category is labelled, further paintings and sculptures are done to exemplify it, as if to order.* The procedure differs from the one that produced old names for literary and artistic genres: sonnet, epic, novel, fresco. These names are neutral, they have never dictated how a new work should go. An epic would have to deal with large events in a narrative spirit of some splendour. A sonnet would probably be a love poem. But neither of these genres binds the poet to an attitude: his love poem may be affectionate or bitter. But an Absurdist play is written as such, as if it were partly written in advance. The existence of a category invites an artist to exemplify it or to exacerbate it; either way, he compromises himself.§ In turn, a new Absurdist play becomes marketable on the precedent of other plays in the same category, so long as the interest in it holds. When the category is sufficiently recognised, it can be alluded to, and imitated for mundane purposes. So we have Mondrian-type wallpapers, Picasso-type tiles, Pollock-type linoleum, Absurdist jokes.

*Craig Raine has written a poem called 'A Martian Sends a Letter Home', a nice poem that practises the mild conceit of looking at things from a slightly odd angle. So now, with a little help from space invaders, there is a category called 'Martian Poetry' which is used to house artificially induced obliquities.

§A more genial possibility: that the name can be taken to indicate the type, of which certain works are the more or less imperfect embodiments. A playwright could try to write another Absurdist play by

76

Stanley Cavell has noted another aspect of management. Such phrases as Action Painting, Pop Art, Absurdist Drama, and Body Art not only make possible a new response, but join in creating it: even when the response has been elicited, the phrases are still *claiming that all the other plays in the same category fail to approach the ideal type denoted by the name.*

required so that it may be maintained. Often, he says, it's hard to know whether the interest is sustained primarily by the work of art or by what can be said about it. The words are no longer tested by how useful they are. In this way, criticism will protect its art against criticism; presumably by confining the discussion to the transaction between the category – Absurdist Drama, say – its exemplification in the particular work – *The Bald Prima Donna* – and your recognition that this is what is going on. The name makes sure that the work will be recognised not (or not necessarily) for what it is, but for the category it fills: this recognition is perhaps as far as one's relation to the work is meant to go.

It's rare to find a critical discrimination between one Action Painting and another. The experience seems to begin and end with the recognition that the work is, indeed, an Action Painting. There is nothing to prevent critical discrimination from taking place. The label is not a veto. But the label gives the viewer, if anything, too much, it pacifies him too soon. To see a poem or a picture as fulfilling a category is to reach a premature sense of it. Naming or labelling is important because it is the most effective means of making something familiar, and familiarity is necessary if the arts are to be managed. The snag is that the familiarity comes too soon, the label imposes local clarity by ridding the work of its mystery and releasing the viewer from his hesitation. But it's hard to make this point without giving the impression that I want people to remain hesitant or insecure forever. I want them to postpone their security. Most cultural forces are working toward making the arts comfortably familiar. The problem is how to break off the impression of familiarity in time to let the force of the artistic vision come through.

T.W. Adorno has an essay 'On the Fetish-Character in Music and the Regression of Listening', which touches on this question. He is concerned with the sociology of pop music, which he calls – he published it in 1938 – commercial music. He doesn't bother to distinguish its various kinds or levels. Commercial music, for Adorno, is music 'intended for consumption', it converts the listener into the consumer. Such music, he argues, goes along with the reduction of people to silence, the dying out of speech as expression, the inability to communicate in any genuine sense at all: 'it inhabits the pockets of silence that develop between people moulded by anxiety, work, and undemanding docility.' He would certainly regard *Top of the Pops* as a symptom of an appalling illness at large. But Adorno's most interesting point is that the question of liking or disliking a piece of commercial music doesn't really arise. If you try to find out who likes a particular pop song, you find that liking and disliking are beside the point or at least that no reasons can be given. 'The familiarity of the music is a surrogate for the quality ascribed to it: to like it is almost the same thing as to recognise it.' Now I think this is still true. It is recognition which explains why, at a pop concert, the loudest applause comes at the beginning rather than at the end of a well-known song. People may of course be anticipating the pleasure they're going to get, but the further source of pleasure is the recognition that a famous song is to be sung now by its famous singer. When Sinatra sings 'My Way' or when James Galway starts playing 'Annie's Song', the applause is warmer than anything earned in the event by the performance. The audience wants Galway to play for them what he is already famous for playing for others: to be present on such an occasion is the richest gratification of the event.

Adorno assumes that familiarity in this sense is contemptible. Or rather, that when liking and disliking have been replaced by spontaneities of recognition, capitalism and commodity-culture have won yet again. I don't agree. Not every experience calls for critical judgement. If it did, none of us could meet the challenge. It's good economy that makes many of our actions automatic or habitual. Proust said that habit is a second nature which keeps us in ignorance of our first and is free of its cruelties and enchantments. If we had to think of walking instead of walking by habit, we would exhaust ourselves by the proliferation of those efforts. Habit lets us reserve our energy for the tasks that need it.

Adorno makes a more telling point when he argues that familiarity ousts the less familiar work. The star system applies to works as much as to their performers. Accepted classics undergo a process of selection that has little to do with quality. Indeed, the situation is far more acute now than it was in 1938. Books are now sold on the supermarket principle; they are given a certain shelf-time. If they are sold immediately, they are ordered again; if not, they are removed, returned to the warehouse, or remaindered.

But a more difficult question arises from a consideration of the management of the arts. Patronage, as the major force in socialising the arts, is incompatible with privacy; it knows experience only as the experience of a group, the larger the better. Think of the most famous instances of patronage in the past few years: the Tutankhamen Exhibition at the British Museum, the Picasso in various places, including the Museum of Modern Art in New York. These were vast public occasions, preceded by immense publicity advertising each event as unique, which it was. Thousands of people saw these exhibitions, but I doubt if any of them saw the paintings or the Tutankhamen items in anything like satisfactory conditions. Queues formed, the crowds had to be controlled, people had to be moved through the gallery at a certain speed. The major constituent of anyone's experience must have been merely the sense of taking part in a big public event with thousands of similarly organised people. No one could have got more from the Picasso than a sense of his extraordinary energy: all those paintings, all those styles. I found it impossible to look at any one painting with the concentration it required. Perhaps the patrons didn't want more, the event was a public gesture, a seal of approval on an accredited culture. The horror of Picasso's paintings, as much as their power, was neutralised, made to comport itself for an occasion essentially civic. Picasso's ferocity didn't stand a chance against the embrace of a cherishing society.

The purpose of such patronage is to reconcile art to a cultural life which is presented as lavish and comfortable. Society never offers to change itself or to take on any of the attributes of art; the invitation always goes the other way. After all, the arts are not necessary; you can keep body and soul together without them. But if they are not necessary, society at least recognises that they are desirable and they can be made to stand for luxuriousness otherwise unattainable. So they are brought into society as glamorous objects, conspicuous proof that the society that contains them is intrinsically fine.* To present them in this way you have to give them a place in daily life; by reporting their activities in newspapers; by employing critics. You can also go in the same direction by attaching to the universities schools of theatre, the visual arts, film, music, and dance. This procedure accustoms the artist to a system which takes naturally to courses, timetables, seminars, and so forth. It's hard to retain a sense of the mystery of art when you have given the artist an office and called him a professor.

*Further: what is important to the patron is to draw the arts toward the centre which he already inhabits: the city. It is no surprise to learn from Robert Hutchison's study of the Arts Council that two-thirds of the British Government's budget for the arts and well over one-third of the Council's expenditure are

Five or six years ago William Golding talked about being the author of *Lord of the Flies*. He felt happy enough about it, but ironic about its official con- | *allocated to the arts in London.*

sequences. 'For better or worse,' he said, 'my work is now indissolubly wedded to the educational world: I am the raw material of an academic light industry. The books that have been written about my books have made a statue of me, fixed in one not very decorative gesticulation, a po-faced image too earnest to live with.'

Golding rightly insists that he is not a statue but a moving target: he has other books to write, he is still changing. He hasn't said anything about *Lord of the Flies* in its character as a set text. He says that the theme of the book is 'grief, sheer grief, grief, grief, grief'; and he leaves it to us to wonder how much of that theme survives the incorporation of the book in an educational system; the teaching of it and the learning of it for examination requirements. After such knowledge, what forgiveness?

But the most serious effect of the management of the arts is that the criteria to be enforced, if any are enforced at all, are managerial, not aesthetic. Since a bourgeois liberal society doesn't know what is true, it pretends to know it and settles rather for what is effective. The question of what is true has become unspeakable, but an air of seriousness can still be achieved by switching from truth to effectiveness. When that word is used, it's thought impertinent to ask what is the nature of the effect. The main point about saying that someone is effective is that it praises the means without reference to the end: it's attached to images and gestures without saying anything about the totality they serve.

What I have in mind as aesthetic criteria, as distinct from effectiveness of a managerial kind, are at least suggested by a passage in Coleridge's *Biographia Literaria*, where he says that 'our genuine admiration of a great poet is a continuous undercurrent of feeling; it is everywhere present, but seldom anywhere as a separate excite-ment.'* That last phrase of Coleridge's reminds me that a society that goes in for diversity and interprets every change as if it manifested a profound spirit at work in our service is likely to be content with separate excitements. Effectiveness may be gained rather by local stimulations than by any continuity of purpose. I don't believe that the big exhibitions, like the Japan Exhibition at the Royal Academy, arise from anyone's decision that we should be alerted to a sense

*A superb modern instance of Coleridgean criticism is Arlene Croce's description of Maurice Béjart's choreography: 'Béjart technique is mannerism surrounded by mystification. It is Paolo Bortoluzzi forever folding his legs into passé from a high

80

of the particular civilisation involved. Each one of them could be replaced by another, with similar publicity, souvenirs and charter flights, and the intentions of the patrons would be equally well served. It could just as well be Indonesia as Japan, Magritte rather than Picasso, the Incas rather than Tutankhamun. The choice is arbitrary.

The standard argument about patronage, that it supports only what is safe, comfortably dead or respectable, may be true but it's beside the point. Patronage is now the practice of management, and management is concerned with method. What is managed doesn't affect the quality of the management, so the choice of one thing rather than another isn't crucial. The point is to show how effective its methods can be.

So what can the artist do to mitigate the worst features of domestication? It opens up some possibilities if his work is sufficiently unpleasant to fend off the warmest excesses of goodwill; if it has the unpleasantness which T.S. Eliot ascribed to Blake's poetry as a mark of its greatness. Samuel Beckett has said that 'art is the apotheosis of solitude'; he has also quoted Schopenhauer's definition of the artistic procedure as 'the contemplation of the world independently of the principle of reason'; and has noted that Dostoevsky 'states his characters without explaining them'. Now Beckett has won all the prizes, but his work is such that it is hard to domesticate: it is never far away from an uncivic grimace or an unassimilable brooding over death. Society has of course taken possession of Beckett's plays and novels, but only up to the point at which their refusing power asserts itself; which is quite early on. In the end, the techniques of management will kidnap any work of art. However churlish the artist, bureaucracy will gather him into its embrace. But the end can be postponed, and there is merit in postponing it.

extension in second, but it is also the cult of Paolo Bortoluzzi doing it. It is Jorge Donn in perpetual fondu, curving his naked belly and parking one foot on the other shin, but it is also the cult of that belly and foot and shin. It is Maina Gielgud turning in her knees and her toes, it is Suzanne Farrell shouldering her leg to 180 degrees or dipping into arabesque penchée or doing split kicks or doing anything, so long as it is to 180 degrees, and it is the cult of the grotesque in the female dance. If dancers have freedom in this company, it is the freedom to drain themselves with monotonous self-repetition. On that basis, it's easy enough to attract a following; these foolish things remind me of you.'

Commentary

Anyone who proposes to manage the arts can claim at least this justification, that the arts are themselves ways of managing more primitive impulses. Form is management: or if you want to think of it rhetorically, it is a paper chase in which the artist carefully drops bits of paper, arbitrarily, as it seems, but not sufficiently arbitrarily to prevent a competent initiate from picking up the trail and sensing the master's direction. The master, in other words, leads the initiate a dance that, seen from the vantage point of a successful conclusion, can be regarded as having been merry. What more piquant, as a form of management, than that the manager should arouse one's desires, frustrate them, thus intensifying them, and eventually relent sufficiently to satisfy them; ideally, just when the victim is on the point of deleting the whole episode, as in rage? Lévi-Strauss has maintained that:

> the musical emotion springs precisely from the fact that at each moment the composer withholds or adds more or less than the listener anticipates on the basis of a pattern that he thinks he can guess, but that he is incapable of wholly divining because of his subjection to a dual periodicity: that of his respiratory system, which is determined by his individual nature, and that of the scale, which is determined by his training.

Aesthetic enjoyment, he goes on to say:

> is made up of this multiplicity of excitements and moments of repose, of expectations disappointed or fulfilled beyond anticipation – a multiplicity resulting from the challenges made by the work and from the contradictory feeling it arouses that the tests it is subjecting us to are impossible, at the same time as it prepares to provide us with the marvellously unpredictable means of coping with them.

You may say that this account makes the composer sound less like a manager than like a coach, encouraging his athlete, goading him, by an elaborate system of pains and pleasures, sticks and carrots. True; but that would only mean that the application of managerial techniques and criteria to the arts is compromised by its simplicity, it is not complicated enough to stay interesting.

In any case, under the heading of 'managing the arts' we are dealing with a form of the larger theme of nature and culture. Culture is the managing of nature, a formula not at all undermined by any equivocations which have been attached to it in modern anthropology. It is not clear in Lévi-Strauss, for instance, whether the opposition of nature and culture which he has used in several books is substantive or methodological. *La Pensée sauvage* may be a turning point, because there he passes from axioms of substance to axioms of method, but in later books it is not clear what status he ascribes, at any moment, to nature and to culture. Does he believe in what the words refer to, or merely use these concepts heuristically?

For my purpose, it doesn't matter. One of the intellectual tendencies of our time is to extend the range of culture to the point at which virtually everything is regarded as cultural and hardly anything as natural. If you start with DNA, and work the ideas of heredity and genetic coding for all they are worth and a little more for good measure, you are left with virtually nothing in the bin called nature. No matter. There is no need for me to quarrel about the demarcation of nature and culture. It wouldn't trouble me if the motives I call, for convenience, natural were to be designated, by someone else, cultural: the obligation would fall on him, then, to distinguish further between motives more or less primitive or more or less developed. If I hit someone and he screams, is the scream natural or cultural? If, on another occasion, he contemplates his own life and emits a scream, is that scream natural or cultural? None of these considerations affects my argument or delays my concession, as follows: the strongest justification for those who would manage the arts is not only that the arts themselves are forms of management but that language is a form of management.

Setting aside the question of demarcation, then, I resort to Nietzsche's *The Birth of Tragedy* and to one of his 'Untimely Meditations' on our theme, which can be given as either (a) the understanding of culture as techniques for managing natural impulses or (b) the understanding of aesthetic forms as ways of acknowledging natural or primitive impulses while leading them a dance, merry or not, toward more accredited patterns of life. In *The Birth of Tragedy* Apollo and Dionysus, whatever character each of them possesses in other contexts and different bodies of lore, are defined as opposing forces. It is in the context of opposition that each is fixed or personified. Dionysus is a god of nature, associated with forces biological and violent, orgiastic mysteries, with everything that refuses to be civilised. Apollo is the god of civilisation: if he were linguistic, he would be the perfectly formed sentence, self-possessed in its transparency. Dionysus wants not to possess himself but to lose himself in an ecstasy in which he and nature are one and the same: the methods of ecstasy are intoxication, sexuality, the Dionysiac music and dance, the dithyramb in which the barriers between man and nature are over-whelmed.

As he appears in the *Bacchae*, Dionysus is wild, god of a maddened group, people who drive themselves out of civilisation by wine, drugs, dismemberment. Modern versions of the Dionysiac include the forces active in bullfights, cockfights, rock concerts, wrestling, charismatic revival meetings. In Nietzsche, tragedy is the form in which Dionysus and Apollo are reconciled. The Dionysiac music, by itself, would be unbearable, because it would defeat culture and shatter the necessary limits implied in character and individuality. The Apolline hero is a hero because he takes upon himself the Dionysiac experience and, not at all transcending it, incorporates it in himself, reconstituting his experience now as form and beauty. In *The Greeks and the Irrational* E.R. Dodds remarks that Dionysus was a popular god, and that he was suppressed eventually because he was alien to the aristocratic ethos of the Homeric hero. But this has to be set beside Nietzsche's argument, in the untimely meditation on Homer, that the Greeks allowed for an Apolline incorpora-tion of Dionysus, and did not try to suppress him:

> The delight in drunkenness, delight in cunning, in revenge, in envy, in slander, in obscenity – in everything which was recognised by the Greeks as human and therefore built into the structure of society and custom: the wisdom of their institutions lies in the absence of any gulf between good and evil, black and white. Nature, as it reveals itself, is not denied but only ordered, limited to specified days and religious cults. That is not the root of all spiritual freedom in the ancient world; the ancients sought a moderate release of natural forces, not their destruction and denial.

So what of modern Dionysus?

Bourgeois society fears the collapse of individuation, since the basis of its ideology is the psychological identity of each individual, vouched for in his consciousness. What such consciousness is supposed to verify is that each of us is, indeed, a separate entity, but also a congenial part of culture through his membership of family, group, state, humanity. We are not supposed to hanker after an aboriginal state of union with nature, as if culture had never happened. Drink and drugs are deemed to be harmful for many reasons but mainly because they remove the cultural distinction between a man and the nature from which he has been rescued. Apollo must win. Each society recognises that there are Dionysiac forces at large, and it makes some provision for them. The carnival of Fasching in Germany is a few days of tumult and licence followed by Lenten rectitude. Public entertainments, sports, including blood sports, motor racing, and sporadic limited wars are provided, as far as possible under controlled conditions. Rock concerts are allowed, but heavily policed and confined to a limited space. But sometimes the provision for the release of violence is not enough: hence the shock expressed by respectable people when, in England, a soccer match is followed by mayhem or, in any country, when a riot is set off by a cause absurdly trivial in itself. Hence, too, the equivocations about pornographic fiction and films: are they deplorable because they show that the domesticating zeal of society does not work well enough, since many people evidently want images of violence and cruelty; or are they somehow acceptable because otherwise these impulses would break out in a deadlier form?

One point seems clear. If we continue extending the definition of culture so that it covers virtually the whole of experience, leaving nothing to nature, we will make it impossible for ourselves to understand violence and obscenity except as failures of 'the system'. It would be wiser to regard culture as a partial and improbable transformation of natural impulse rather than a comfortable norm. That way, manifestations of violence could be considered without the normal accompaniment of shock, horror, and insult. Why do we bother so much to save appearances? Think of the fame and aura of the Rolling Stones. Young people must be in acute need of the sentiment of being natural if they are appeased, as they evidently are, by the most blatant mimicry of Dionysiac frenzy which is all that Mick Jagger offers. Jagger is no more Dionysiac than Robert Redford is, so a society must be far gone in anaemia if it mistakes his mimicries for the real Dionysiac thing.

It is significant that these mimicries and pretences are offered in popular music, because the Dionysiac forces have always expressed themselves in music and dance. The Rolling Stones used words, they sang songs, but the words were of no account: what counted was the event, the repetitive beat, the scream, the gesture, the leaping about on the stage. Pop words, such as they are, are designed to humiliate the official processes of speech; the audience responds to a fury in the words, but not to the words. It is also part of the act that the stage gyrations don't pretend to any skill; because skill would suggest conformity to the requirements of dance, an accredited institution like any other. Pop culture recoils from the bourgeois virtues demanded in the arts, the laborious exercises which produce pianists, violinists, French horn players, ballet-dancers, opera singers: these are scorned because they sustain the official institutions of cultural life. By definition, they do not rely upon spontaneity, whim, or other forces which offer seeming immediacies of gesture in preference to hard-won skill. Managerial techniques come into force in the form of advertising, gossip, the cult of personality, and all the other rigmaroles which add up to a 'media event'. At that stage, with carefully calculated belatedness, pop culture finds it worth its while to join the bourgeois ideology it pretends to despise. All roads lead to Wardour Street.

The strongest justification of management is that language itself is managerial. This is well recognised in *The Renaissance* where Pater refers to the way in which our flickering impressions, unstable and inconsistent, seem to become objects because of 'the solidity with which language invests them'. In language, it is almost impossible to bear in mind that there is not a name for everything. Humanists like to think that everything has a name, lest they have to conclude that some things or some events lie beyond our knowing. Much of this sentiment concentrates upon the security of naming. Wittgenstein said, admittedly in a passage much disputed, that 'it will often prove useful in philosophy to say to ourselves: naming something is like attaching a label to a thing.' Attaching a label to a thing doesn't necessarily exert a claim to full knowledge of it, but rather to a ready practical use of it, and enough knowledge of it to make the use possible. The issue is complicated but the case is not at all undermined by a later passage in the *Philosophical Investigations* where Wittgenstein says: 'where our language suggests a body and there is none: there, we should like to say, is a *spirit*.'

The part of this I want is his acknowledgement that our language does indeed suggest bodies: nothing comes more 'naturally' to language than to do this. I think Lévi-Strauss, in the 'Overture' to *The Raw and the Cooked*, got this thought expressed sooner rather than later, for fear it would dog him if unexpressed. If it were possible to prove, he says:

that the apparent arbitrariness of the mind, its supposedly spon-

86

taneous flow of inspiration, and its seemingly uncontrolled inventiveness imply the existence of laws operating at a deeper level, we would inevitably be forced to conclude that when the mind is left to commune with itself and no longer has to come to terms with objects, it is in a sense reduced to imitating itself as object; and that since the laws governing its operations are not fundamentally different from those it exhibits in its other functions, it shows itself to be of the nature of a thing among things.

If you wanted to reach this conclusion, or at least to get it out in the open, you would have to assume that words make whatever they refer to appear to be objects. You would then add the notion that the mind can only commune with itself by communing with words, on the analogy of fondling objects. Then you could complete the transaction by making the mind take its character from the object-like character of the words it deals with. A milder version of this would be Charles Morris's argument in his *Signs, Language and Behaviour* that all moral ideas are products of language.

William Empson takes this notion up in his *Structure of Complex Words*, asking 'whether we would alter our moral ideas if we realised what language was doing to us.' What language is mostly doing to us is supplying a set of bins into which our feelings are supposed to be thrown; thrown, rather than delicately placed, because it is something we're meant to do as if spontaneously. If the particular bin doesn't seem to be the right one, we take time to look for another, but normally the readiness of the bin urges us to be satisfied with it. Empson's point, answering Morris's behaviourism, is that 'most people, whether educated or not, are tolerably clear about "emotive" words; if they don't feel as the word tells them to do they recognise a disagreement for which they feel they have grounds, and they "get round" the word by irony or something.'

Empson doesn't dispute that words tend to administer our feelings by offering us fairly simple bins for them: what he adds is that when we feel the bin isn't the right one and yet no other offers itself, we use the bin with mental reservations: it corresponds to our using a word but qualifying our use with a smirk, a smile, a recognisably false accent, or whatever. In any case it is not necessary to accept the notion of atomic sentences as mirroring atomic facts, an idea the Vienna Circle received from Wittgenstein's *Tractatus*, if all we want to observe is that language tends to divide our experience into segments that have the appearance of objects. The point is that this procedure tends to give people not only descriptions of their feelings which may or may not fit: it gives them conclusions before thay have felt the need of them. Which is what administration does. Administrators don't merely meet a situation which has been causing trouble. They devise a system of management: once the system is in place, it needs to occupy itself, if only to keep itself in trim and develop its capacities.

What then do managers think of the arts? I have suggested that they mostly think of them as things like any other, to be administered in much the same way. If they have in view a politics or even a sociology, they regard the arts as safety-valves, useful and perhaps even necessary, given the character of the social machine. Some poets – I'll give an example in a moment – are ready to settle for this analogy. And certainly it has many advantages over Lévi-Strauss's habit of dealing with the mind as an object among objects. Nobody would want that habit unless he were terrified of the flux or the promiscuous merging of one sensation into another which he would take to be the only alternative. In *Tristes Tropiques* there is a revealing passage where Lévi-Strauss makes fun of his early teachers for reading Bergson rather than Saussure, and for not taking Freud seriously when he told them that 'the most apparently emotional behaviour, the least rational procedures and so-called pre-logical manifestations' are 'at the same time the most meaningful'.

> Rejecting the Bergsonian acts of faith and circular arguments which reduced beings and things to a state of mush the better to bring out their ineffability, I came to the conclusion that beings and things could retain their separate values without losing the clarity of outline which defines them in relationship to each other and gives an intelligible structure to each. . . . Knowledge is based neither on renunciation nor on barter; it consists rather in selecting *true* aspects, that is, those coinciding with the properties of my thought. Not, as the neo-Kantians claimed, because my thought exercises an inevitable influence over things, but because it is itself an object. Being 'of this world', it partakes of the same nature as the world.

Now there are so many flaws in this argument that it would take a disproportionate amount of time to unravel them. In what sense is my thought an object? If my thought is an object, is my thinking an object? Even if my thought were an object, what would it mean to say that it partakes of the same nature as the world? What is that nature? Is it matter or energy or what? And in any case what is the source of security, or how do I know that I have selected true aspects, merely because I deem my thinking to partake of the same nature as the world?

The questionable sense in which my thought partakes of the same nature as the world gives, in fact, no authority whatever to my thinking. My thinking could be crazy and still retain whatever partaking nature it ever had. It seems more reasonable to distinguish my thought from 'the world', whatever that phrase means, while making the easy concession that anything that exists shares existence with everything else that exists. The merit of the theory of the arts as safety-valve is that it keeps them within the syntax of the engine while giving them a special function. It doesn't exaggerate their function, since the inaugurating force and momentum of the engine don't issue from the valve. The best text I know on this matter is Empson's poem 'Your Teeth are Ivory Towers', which he wrote in 1940 when people worried about the value of whatever they were doing.

Empson's poem answers those critics, like F.R. Leavis, who denounced escapist poetry. Escapist poets were only talking to themselves, like infants. Empson says, against this, that talking to yourself isn't such a bad thing. Goodwill, even when it isn't directed to anyone in particular, is agreeable and positive. But in any case:

> The safety valve alone
> Knows the worst truth about the engine; only the child
> Has not yet been misled.

Empson has always had a lot of time for this neo-Wordsworthian truth about children, wise before the event. His gloss on the lines I've quoted says that 'the relation of the artist to his society may include acting as safety valve or keeping the fresh eye, etc., of the child, and therefore can't be blamed out of hand for escapism or infantilism.' Still, to say that poetry is like a child's babble makes a concession as much as a claim. From a public point of view, the child is just a pretty form of anarchy. The poem takes up the question and says, ruefully, that it was feasible to carry anarchy so long as the official values of a society were sustained; by Christianity, for instance, or by secular power:

We could once carry anarchy, when we ran
Christ and the magnificent milord
As rival pets; the thing is, if we still can

Lacking either.

That is: 'it is not clear that in the new great machine or mass societies, which accept neither ideal, there is the same room for the artist.' Empson means, I think, that the poet's anarchy had its meaning in a particular relation to the order it challenged. It accords with my own feeling that the best way in which an artist can be present is in conflict with his society. Conflict, in that formula, means a specific engagement, necessarily now on the margin of a society which typically likes to pretend that it has no margin at all, every square inch of the space of experience being already filled.

Empson's doubt about the artist's place in a mass society arises from the situation which Ortega y Gasset described in 1930 in *The Revolt of the Masses*. Ortega's mass man has no interest in distinctions between text and margin, or between one form of life and another. He has no preference, except for winning. Nicola Chiaromonte's answer to Ortega, in *The Worm of Consciousness*, takes the form of saying that 'the problem of the masses is the problem of the real or apparent impotence of the intellectual and the teacher in mass society': it is the teacher or the intellectual who has yielded to the quantitative and numerical values which have produced mass man. Empson's poem should be read in the space between Ortega and Chiaromonte. He evidently thinks that there is still a point to the arts, but his way of making this claim is exorbitant:

the spry arts
Can keep a steady hold on the controls

By seeming to evade. But if it parts
Into incommunicable spacetimes, few
Will hint or ogle, when the stoutest heart's

Best direct yell will never reach . . .

Incommunicable spacetimes are, presumably, mass society. Not even Donne could hope to deal with such a thing. Hinting, ogling, and evading are the gestures of fictiveness and style. What the controls are, on which the spry arts can keep a steady hold, is not clear: if the arts are good at knowing the best and the worst, that doesn't give them competence in worldly action or a seat at the conference table. They are 'effective' only within the parentheses of fiction. The poem ends with a typical stance on Empson's part: his advice is to do the best you can, live by the unofficial code of talk and goodwill:

> He who tries
> Talk must always plot and then sustain,
> Talk to himself until the star replies,
>
> Or in despair that it could speak again
> Assume what answers any wits have found
> In evening dress on rafts upon the main,
> Not therefore uneventful or soon drowned.

I take him as saying that even if civilisation has sunk, like the *Titanic*, it remains for the poet, whether or not he can make a philosophy to justify what he does, to keep things going, gathering up the spars and fragments and living with them as best he can. Empson is interested in philosophical systems, but even more in the Tory possibility of getting along without one. The answers any wits have found will last, he hopes, even if society doesn't care for them.

Empson's account of the relation between the artist and society is desperate, to the point at which it develops the courage of despair. It could be argued that mass society is already well on the way to fulfilling itself. Mechanisation, bureaucracy, the increasing complexity of technology and scientific specialisation are, as Chiaromonte says, typical phenomena of mass society today, 'yet they seem to vitiate the authority of the individual, as well as the democratic power of the majority, in favour of an anonymous principle of organisation and discipline.' If this is the case, the artist can't hope for any privileges from mass society, or even from the concession of a marginal status. Empson's poem speaks of the artist as if he might still be wiry enough to hold a place for himself, even if things go from the present bad to a future worse. But that would amount to a claim to work in conditions of freedom, not of the necessity in which everyone works in a mass society. Such a society won't recognise the need of a safety valve.

The liberty the arts have claimed for themselves has taken many forms. My argument is that modern bourgeois society isn't interested in constraining the artist as much as in domesticating him. Empson's feeling is – and here Chiaromonte's book tells the same story – that a mass society won't have any need of the artist, and presumably won't bother even to domesticate his mystery. But even if the conditions are pointing toward a mass society, it is not yet in place: societies, at least in the West, have not yet ditched – even in academic theory – the values we think of as liberal or democratic. So it is still possible for artists to think of themselves as slightly but blessedly marginal, as if domestication or nullification were not yet complete. The proof of this sentiment is that the artist still thinks of his work as being slightly aslant from the appearances it alludes to. I am thinking of 'The Wall and its Books' in which Borges establishes the aesthetic virtue somewhere to one side of its official reference, as in aesthetic forms which, he says, 'have their virtue in themselves and not in any conjectural "content"':

> Music, states of happiness, mythology, faces belaboured by time, certain twilights and certain places try to tell us something, or have said something we should have missed, or are about to say something; this imminence of a revelation which does not occur is, perhaps, the aesthetic phenomenon.

What is common to all these instances, if we can call them that for the moment? Music is pure form, so that if we think of content it is only to feel that it has been refined out of every material existence. States of happiness are those, too, in which the state suffuses whatever content it has had. Mythology tells not facts but their ideal form. Faces belaboured by time keep their secret, as Empson said of Hamlet, by showing that they have one: they do not coincide with their lineaments. Twilights and certain places are not what they seem but what they allow each of us to deem them to be. Finally, the imminence of a revelation which does not occur, the veil that continues to tremble, forever still to be enjoyed: it is a question of tense, in which the present leans from itself toward a future indefinitely proposed and postponed.

The tendency of 'the aesthetic phenomenon' to veer from its official reference has a corresponding grammar. The clearest account of it known to me is in I.A. Richards's *Principles of Literary Criticism*, where he says that 'there is a suppressed conditional clause implicit in all poetry':

> If things were such and such then . . . and so the response develops. The amplitude and fineness of the response, its sanction and authority, in other words, depend upon this freedom from actual assertion in all cases in which the belief is questionable on any ground whatsoever.

I don't see why the qualification – 'in which the belief is questionable on any ground whatsoever' – is required. Why remove the conditional clause merely because you happen to agree with the sentiment well enough to accept its assertion? Richards's theory would be more coherent if a suppressed conditional clause were to be implicit in all poetry, and indeed in all works of art. In poetry, this would allow us to take every statement as if it were made by a character, one of several, in a play. Any claim to truth would reside in the 'play' as a whole, not in anything a particular character said. In a poem, the suppressed conditional clause would be represented by the formality of the poem. The space of a painting is similarly conditional, it does not coincide with the common space on which people build houses, roads, or railways.

In music, too, time is not common time. Comparing myth with music, Lévi-Strauss starts with the remark that each requires a temporal dimension in which to unfold:

> But this relation to time is of a rather special nature: it is as if music and mythology needed time only in order to deny it. Both, indeed, are instruments for the obliteration of time. Below the level of sounds and rhythms, music acts upon a primitive terrain, which is the physiological time of the listener; this time is irreversible and therefore irredeemably diachronic, yet music transmutes the seg-ment devoted to listening to it into a synchronic totality, enclosed within itself. Because of the internal organization of the musical work, the act of listening to it immobilizes passing time; it catches and enfolds it as one catches and enfolds a cloth flapping in the wind. It follows that by listening to music, and while we are listening to it, we enter into a kind of immortality.

I wonder. I have just listened to a performance of Beethoven's Sonata for Violin and Piano in C minor. It is true that the time I spent listening to it did not feel 'the same' as the time immediately before or after. But I did not feel that the music immobilised time, even passing time. The experience of listening to the music was temporal. Time was not denied or transcended. In that sense, I don't understand Lévi-Strauss's saying that the time of the music was 'transmuted' into a synchronic totality, if he means me to take seriously the spatial form he implies, or even if he has in mind that the music happens 'simultaneously'. The sonata didn't; it enacted a relation to time such that the themes, cadences, repetitions, and rhythms seemed to want to realise themselves in a time enhanced by

93

that striving, and by the momentum of it. It was the difference between Chronos and Kairos, between mere passing time and time animated by value and power.

Susanne K. Langer's *Feeling and Form* is helpful here in its account of the difference between our normal categories and the nuances of them which constitute the elements of the arts. She is concerned with the ways in which the work of art stands out from the distractions that compete with it. Her theory of the arts is derived from her theory of music: its main defect is that it 'reduces' all the arts to the condition of music, by smoothing away the factors in any art which amount to distraction or recalcitrance. The result is that the theory doesn't work very well with literature, in which it is impossible to separate a word from the distracting and distracted offices it performs in other contexts. However, Mrs Langer's basic argument is that the elements of art are virtual, as distinct from the actual elements of our ordinary experience, which are involved in many other purposes and settings. Time, for instance. Clock-time is time as pure sequence, its events are indifferent in themselves, and their sole relation one to another is that of succession. Lived time differs from clock-time by virtue of the feelings, interests, and so forth which give it its character. We don't live by the clock. But music 'makes time audible, and its form and continuity sensible'.

It is a limitation, I think, in Mrs Langer's theory that she defines 'virtual' as 'created only for perception'. The definition has the advantage of distinguishing the artistic symbol from other created objects which are created for various purposes and occasions. Perception, indeed, makes the work of art stand out from the distractions that compete with it; or rather, it is the proper response, on the part of the listener or the viewer, to such a quality in the work of art. But it has the disadvantage of implying that the work of art is such that a sustained act of perception will exhaust it, come to the end of its possibilities. I would argue otherwise; if perception comes to the end of the work of art, as distinct from coming to the end of its own patience or energy, so much the worse for the work of art.

This disability in Mrs Langer's theory is accompanied by another one. Music, she says, is a purely auditory illusion; that is, it is offered only to the ear. If she means only the obvious fact that we hear music rather than seeing it or tasting it, well and good. But 'the ear', by itself, could make nothing whatever of music: it is the cooperation of mind and ear which makes sense. But, leaving that aside, Mrs Langer then says that the primary illusion of music 'is the sonorous image of passage, abstracted from actuality to become free and plastic and entirely perceptive'. The last phrase is one too many: free and plastic, yes, but 'entirely perceptive' makes a principle out of a disability. Mrs Langer is not free from the positivism she objects to.

In an Orwellian vision, one might project a mass society such that the nuancing of elements which I have attributed to the arts would be prohibited. Nuanced elements would mean a deflection from the official programmes designed to govern our lives, as in a text without margins. Virtuality would be banned, and the official forms of distraction would be enforced. Engines would be designed as self-regulating, making safety-valves unnecessary.

To sum up, on the question of language as management. Kenneth Burke has observed in *The Rhetoric of Religion* that 'there are four realms to which words may refer.' First: there are words for the natural, for things, physiological conditions and the like, such words as 'tree', 'dog', 'hunger', and 'growth'. These words name the sorts of things and events which would be included in the world even if the ability to use words were to be eliminated from existence. Second: there are words for the socio-political realm, words for social relations, laws, judgements of right and wrong, authority and the like; such words as 'good', 'justice', 'monarchy', 'patrimony'. Third: there are words about words, in the realm of dictionaries, grammar, etymology, philology, rhetoric, aesthetics; such words as 'tone', 'syllable', 'rhyme', 'form', and so forth. These three orders of terms, Burke says, 'should be broad enough to cover the world of everyday experience, the empirical realm for which words are preeminently suited'. But we must also have a fourth order: words for 'the supernatural'. For even if you didn't believe in the supernatural, you would recognise that languages have words for the supernatural. However, our words for the discussion of the supernatural are necessarily borrowed by analogy from our words for the other three orders:

> The supernatural is by definition the realm of the 'ineffable'. And language by definition is not suited to the expression of the 'ineffable'. So our words for the fourth realm . . . are necessarily borrowed from our words for the sorts of things we can talk about literally, our words for the three empirical orders.

So if we were to speak of God, we might refer to God's presence or power, using a natural or physical analogy: or to God the Father, using a socio-political analogy: or to God as Logos or Truth, using a linguistic analogy. To go a little beyond Burke's argument: many of our words for 'the ineffable' are formed by using a corresponding empirical word and denying its limitations, as we speak of immortality not by finding a word precisely for it but by saying that 'it is the opposite of mortality or free from the constraint of mortality.' For the same reason, we say that that which is beyond physics is metaphysics, as that which considers the ultimate ground of criticism is metacriticism. When a poet feels or divines a realm beyond anything that can be specified, he says that 'words after speech, reach into the silence', as if that silence were metaspeech, which it is.

It is evident that language must be forced to go beyond its empirical character. Silence, as we are forced to take the weight of the word in *The Four Quartets*, is a scandal to speech, an offence to the adequacy claimed by the empirical orders of language. What I have called the managerial motive in language is, more desperately, the insistence of those who use it that there is nothing it cannot name. Poetic language refutes this observation by transgressing it. Bourgeois language insists on finding signifieds for every signifier, and containing the entire field within the rule of law: the law is the homogeneity of signification. Julia Kristeva has suggested a psychoanalytic understanding of this law and of poetic language as its infringement. The subject of poetic language, she says in *Desire in Language*, 'continually but never definitively assumes the thetic function of naming, establishing meaning and signification, which the paternal function represents. . . . Son is permanently at war with father, not in order to take his place, or even to endure it . . . but rather to signify what is untenable in the symbolic, nominal, paternal function.' So the son-subject is driven into every form of excess, fending off the only fate his society has arranged for him, that of being a sign.

What, then, have I been talking about? Just this: if experience is, in practice, divided into official and unofficial, authoritative and occult; what corresponds to this division, in language, is the distinction between discourse, with its official diction, and the several poetries, with their several 'contradictions'. It is the aim of management to accommodate every apparent contradiction within a standard diction by neutralising the offensive words.

FIVE

THE ANXIOUS OBJECT

Two years ago the critic Marina Vaizey wrote an essay on the language of art criticism in which she reflected severely on those dictionaries of art which, as she said, 'do not criticize their subjects so much as praise them'.* But the most revealing passage in her essay reported that in a London art gallery one day she came upon what she described as 'a middle-aged pair doing the art-gallery swoop'. In the swoop

Lady Vaizey is the resident art-critic on The Sunday Times *(London).*

you look at a painting and then bend down to see its title and the painter's name. The middle-aged pair were bending down to look at an electrical fitting, a complex of wires and plugs which they evidently took for a work of art. They were searching for the label. 'So disorientated had this couple become,' Lady Vaizey commented, 'so uncertain as to what was art and what wasn't, that their eyes were taking in the sculptural possibilities of electrical plugs and wires while looking for the label that would validate their perceptions.' 'I can't see what this is called,' one said to the other as Lady Vaizey passed by.

The conclusions Lady Vaizey drew from this episode seem to me wrong. She implies that she is free from the bewilderment she ascribes to the middle-aged pair. I don't think she is. She recently reviewed in *The Sunday Times* a work by Joseph Beuys, exhibited in Anthony d'Offay's Gallery in London. It isn't very clear from her account of it that she has any notion of its character, or whether it is a work of art or not. She assures her readers that Beuys is 'a person of the utmost dedication, charm, and sincerity'. 'The effect of Beuys's work has an emotional effect,' she says, bewilderment stunning her sentence. In fact, she is in exactly the same degree of disorientation as the middle-aged pair looking at the wires and plugs, except for one privileged consideration: she knows the artist's name and has already experienced, apparently, his charm.

On the matter of dictionaries of art which do not criticise their subjects so much as praise them, Lady Vaizey is not in a strong position. Some months ago she reviewed an exhibition of Constructivist Art in

97

Britain 1934–1940 and referred to certain 'marvellous carvings, stone and wood, by Henry Moore', some pieces by Barbara Hepworth, and a few of Ben Nicholson's white reliefs. But 'pride of place, even in this company,' she wrote, 'must go to the daring, sizzlingly assured Piet Mondrian "Composition White and Red" (1935).'

It's hard to see how concentration of mind could be compatible with such a sentence, or with Lady Vaizey's recent description of David Hockney as 'an artist of sizzling and attractive intelligence'. Now it is possible to describe a Mondrian painting as 'assured', if you ignore the obsessive sense of experience and the precautionary stance which found their embodiment in his horizontals, verticals, and primary colours; and if you ignore the sundry of experience he felt driven to suppress. But what then remains of the assurance you have ascribed to his composition? In any case what force are we meant to give that word 'sizzlingly', which is evidently designed to drive into sublimity a sentence that began, unpromisingly, with 'pride of place'?

I mention this simply to document my surprise that any art critic can feel exempt, these days, from a sense of incapacity. Several years ago one of the best and most influential critics, Harold Rosenberg, acknowledged that the whole activity of art criticism is confounded. 'The nature of art has become uncertain. At least it is ambiguous. No one can say with assurance what a work of art is – or, more important, what is not a work of art. Where an art object is still present, as in painting, it is what I have called an anxious object: it does not know whether it is a masterpiece or junk.'

So how should we proceed? Rosenberg didn't say, what is obvious, that in many instances the artist's name is essential. A painting by Mondrian is a Mondrian. We look at it, knowing that it takes its place in that category. If you attend a performance of Boulez's 'Structures la', you probably bring to it a general sense of what his name stands for, and perhaps a more specific sense if you have heard two or three of his works. That you are listening to a Boulez rather that a Stockhausen, a Maxwell Davies, or a Steve Reich, is part of the experience.* You may even go to the trouble of reading Gyorgy Ligeti's analysis; in that case you'll know that the system on which Boulez wrote the piece is very elaborate. You won't know whether it is good or not, because Ligeti's analysis is limited to explication. Presumably he thinks it good enough to hold his professional interest, but apart from that consideration

> *What difference would it make if you listened to a Boulez, thinking you were listening to a Stockhausen? A lot; now that the 'persona ising' of artistic experiences complete. It was not always

98

you'll have to wait for the evidence of your ear even to decide whether or not to pursue the question of value.

The artist's name hasn't always been a necessary part of the aesthetic experience. In the sixteenth century the name only indicated the point at which human genius manifested itself: people were far more interested in the continuity of the power of genius than in the individual person marked out to receive it. But since the beginning of the nineteenth century the name has been the focus of attention to the individuality of the artist. Schumann praised Chopin mainly for the unmistakably personal quality of his music, and thought it a mark of Chopin's genius that his music, like a signature, was unlike anyone else's. An aesthetic experience demanded the disclosure of private feeling. Artists who gave up the security and reserve of distance and chose rather to reveal every nuance of their sensibility were rewarded for doing so. Liszt's recitals were lavish in the exchange of emotion. Liberal humanism has identified a work of art with its author and valued the signs of genius uniquely his. Some critics maintain that the age of liberal humanism is past and that reference to an artist's genius is mystification. But the correlation persists. When Andy Warhol was asked how he would recognise a work of art, he said that whatever an artist does is a work of art. When Marcel Duchamp exhibited in a gallery a bottle rack and a snow shovel bought in a hardware shop, it was assumed that he meant to refute the supposed difference between a standard commercial object and a work of art; but the bottle rack and snow shovel were different in one respect, they had been chosen by an artist, his royal hand had touched them. The same applies to Warhol's famous tin of Campbell's soup.

But the difference between the nineteenth and the twentieth century in this regard is that in the nineteenth the work of art was still separable from the artist and it participated in forms and genres to which specific criteria applied. Bottle racks, snow shovels, and soup tins embody intentions and gestures to which criteria don't apply. All you can do with an intention is entertain it. When Rosenberg said that it was no longer possible to say what a work of art is or what is not a work of art, he meant that many works offered as art no longer reveal in themselves the reasons why they are such: they disable critical judgement by being arbitrary. The artist might say: precisely; that is the point, to disable judgement,

thus. Three hundred years ago, people didn't ask — with anything like our insistence — who wrote the work, what's he like? The name of the author became an essential constituent of the work when Romanticism's lyric cry against industrialism was heard as a peculiarly personal challenge.

and force upon people an entirely spectacular experience.

I suppose most people, if asked what art is, would say something along these lines. A work of art is a work designed as such, even when a practical use is primarily intended, as in architecture; it is offered to our perception as a work at once expressive, formal, and unified; offered in the hope of arousing and gratifying our aesthetic sense, our sense of the beautiful in the manifestation of form. The relation between the work of art and the given world may be close or distant. It may be close, as in art which seeks to resemble, refer, allude, or denote; or it may be so distant that it shows more interest in the world as it might be or a world quite different from our own than in the common world given to us in its appearances. Some forms of art, like painting, sculpture, or the novel, are comfortable with the possibility of resemblance: others, like music, are not. The pleasure offered by a work of art is the pleasure of understanding an object for its own sake even though understanding can't be more than partial. A work of art is then admired for various reasons; for durability, in the sense that it has survived, valued by generations of people who in one degree or another have admired it; or it has shown notable power to move a wide range of people, so that it is easy to believe that it testifies to some permanent feature of human life. Or it is, for some reason, unique, even in its imperfection; no one seriously wants to see the Venus de Milo restored, even though several artists have tried to imagine what form its perfection took. Sometimes a work of art is valued for its originality; though there is a critical argument that the appearances of originality are misleading, and that the new is merely the old we have failed to recognise. Sometimes what we admire in a work of art is its perfection, the ease with which it answers the formal problems it has set.

These are the kind of assumptions one makes in a reasonable conversation about art. And they are perfectly reasonable. But when we recite such considerations, we feel that they are archaic to some of the current forms of art. The reason is that they all sustain the idea of the work of art as a privileged object, valued because it is removed from the normal wear-and-tear of daily life as a sign of its status. These works come from a past that seems increasingly remote, and their presence among us is obtrusive. If they are housed in galleries, you have to look at them with special gravity and decorum. There may even be a touch of resentment, that these things have not changed as we have changed.

It is easy to resent the claim a famous work of art makes upon you: all that history, all that glory. Some such feeling may have urged contemporary artists to suppress the privilege of art; so they make their works of art not as durable objects but as events, happenings, or gestures. They want to call attention not to the object but to the processes of art, which reveal themselves best in forms designed not to last; in collages made of bits of paper, all the better if it is newspaper, made to be replaced and forgotten. Still, these are odd feelings. If we revolt against the object, we turn against the past which has granted the privilege. Our sense of the past is intimidating because we feel we have to be loyal to it. Maurice Blanchot has argued that societies like to have finished works of art that can be admired as perfect and whose external immobility can be contemplated in museums and concert halls; they like to have these things so that people may be able to recognise themselves in works of art and feel that there is continuity between past and present. If we don't feel satisfied or comforted when we go to an art gallery, it's probably because we resent the walls of official perfection we are required to admire.

Some years ago Lionel Trilling brought together a number of ideas which bear upon this theme: 'a diminished confidence in mind', which he regarded as typical of our time; 'our diminished awareness of the past', and 'our disaffection from history'. 'Mind is widely discredited', he maintained, 'because it cannot be in an immediate relation to experience, but must always stand merely proximate to it.' He had in view the sentiment which stipulates 'that only those things are real, true, and to be relied on which are experienced without the intervention of rational thought'. The irritating quality of mind is that it always comes after the event, and mostly in the form of a rebuke. The reason why Romantic poets spoke rather of imagination and vision than of mind is that imagination consorts with beginnings, it is spontaneous, creative, it speaks of possibility rather than necessity. William Blake wrote: 'Energy is the only life; it issues from the body; and Reason is the bound and outward circumference of Energy. Energy is eternal delight.' Kant said that genius is 'that innate disposition of the temperament through which nature imposes its law on art.' In other words, genius comes into art as a turbulence in its routine. By the criteria of genius and energy, Mind is bound to appear a tedious necessity. It seems always to play the older brother in experience, if not the heavy father. And among the properties of mind, the most formidable and the most forbidding seems to be the power of judgement and discrimination. Discrimination is the 'delayed satisfaction' of mind, which is itself the delayed satisfaction of experience. No wonder they are hated by those who want their experience to be direct and immediate, without thought of yesterday or the morrow.

These considerations may account for some changes in the status of the several arts. The most popular arts these days are those which provide the most direct access to their experiences. The question of the relative value of the experiences doesn't seem to be raised: it is as if what people want of any experience is chiefly its immediacy, and would settle for experiences which have that quality and nothing much else. Music encourages people to believe that it is possible to dissolve all the tensions involved in personal and social relations, and to enter into the possession of experience so intimately that words are not required. All the better because words are not required.* The appeal of dance is related to an ideal unity of experience, verified by the human body, its animation, gestures, identity, and movement; by the relation between the body and the earth on which it moves. Equally, in dance, the partnering of dancers testifies to a personal and communal sense of life, freed from the tendentiousness of language and the equivocal luxury of entirely private feeling. Music and dance alike hold out the possibility of universal experience, free from the rational necessity which is accepted in speech.

Music is predicated on the belief that we all share the same life, and that it is possible to be present to it, as if prior to all discursive strife, through musical forms, cadences, and rhythms.

In this sense, each art promises particular satisfaction. Painting and sculpture promise the sense of presence, of a thing's being completely at one with itself, fully what it is, without yielding to a demand for explanation. Sculpture in particular promises us a relation to the material world such that it no longer seems primitive or intractable. The same sense is developed more explicitly in architecture, which holds out the possibility of achieving complete harmony between nature and culture; of so being at home in the world that our houses and public buildings will seem as natural as the ground they occupy. Architecture, being a public art, also offers relief from the demands of subjectivity: a successful public building allows us to feel that society is our proper home and that civic life can provide satisfactions, not merely frustrations. Photography appeases the desire to take immediate possession of our experience; not indeed as a whole but as the sum of its separately manageable parts. When life is most keenly felt as miscellaneous and formless, it's a relief to see it under picturesque control, held in focus when it most threatens to fly off in several directions. The importance of the Polaroid camera is that it removes the delay between the experience and its image, increasing the owner's sense of immediate possession.

By these comparisons, literature offers no immediacy at all. Its medium is language, so it is compromised by questions of meaning, definition, and syntax. Literature, for these reasons, is always belated. Language is full of gaps; the gap between a thing and the word for it, the insecurity that remains even when you have settled upon the word, the gap between the words and the system they inhabit. There are poems in which the words seem to revel in their relations to one another, and to neglect their official meanings. There is a use of language which seems opaque rather than transparent. When Eliot writes in 'Gerontion',

What will the spider do,
Suspend its operations, will the weevil
Delay?

there is no point in detaching these questions from their context or expecting that, even in context, they might be answered. But in any case it is impossible to place words close to primary experience. Think of 'automatic writing', which tries to use words in such a way as to forestall the intervention of mind or systematic thought. It is always ludicrous. These gestures have more point as Rorschach episodes in psychology. Or in painting; Robert Klein has pointed out that abstract art implies a way of being in the world as if one had given up relying upon the certainty of objects and the completeness of Nature. That's why the abstract expressionist painter paints before he reflects; because reflection entails recourse to everything he wants to evade, to punish, or to subdue; ideas, objects, the whole apparatus of a given world. So it's not surprising that Surrealism has been more compelling in paint than in words. It's hard to prevent words from referring to other things; they run, as if by nature, to make the kind of sense which is implied in grammar, syntax, and argument. The tendency can be deflected, as in the literature of nonsense, but you have to deform the words, as in Lewis Carroll and Edward Lear, and you have to play fast and loose with syntax, otherwise the words will go straight to their old ways. But paint doesn't harbour a preference for allusion or representation; the relation between paint and canvas is free of grammar, so it is easy to set hand, brush, and paint in motion as if the hand were disconnected from the mind.

It may seem that the attempt to disconnect the hand from the mind is perverse, but it arises from a motive that has been common in the arts at least for the past two hundred years. Jacques Maritain described it by saying that 'Art, once bitten by poetry, longs to be freed from reason.'

The sentence calls upon an ancient tradition in which the artist is associated with divine madness, inspiration, enthusiasm, and ecstasy. Instead of copying nature or the cultured object, he was supposed to trust his genius no matter where it led him. He was more important than any object he painted, because he was inspired. In the story of Pygmalion, the sculptor made an ivory statue of a woman so beautiful that he fell in love with his own creation. But the statue remained cold until Aphrodite took pity on Pygmalion; and one day while pressing the inert statue in his arms he felt the ivory suddenly move; his kisses were returned. The statue had come alive. Reason would have discouraged Pygmalion from such a dreadful art, or would have argued him into a more disinterested sense of his own creation. But reason is extravagant in its own way, it imposes a more stringent degree of order than our experience requires, its talent is administrative rather than creative. The trick is to destroy our devils without destroying our angels. Reason would destroy both sets, just to make sure. So when we talk about the revulsion against reason in the last two hundred years, we can improve its reputation by saying that it is an attempt to speak up for whatever reason would suppress: dreams, the unconscious, the anarchy of pure behaviour, the immediacy of instinct and intuition.

The motive I am describing appears in many forms, some more charming that the rest. One of the most charming appears in John Cage, a composer who entertains noise as willingly as silence; he is quiet by temperament and now by conviction. When Richard Kostelanetz asked Cage why he composed, since music is merely 'random sound experience', he answered: 'The first thing you have to do is not ask the question "why". Look at your environment, which you are enjoying, and see if it asks why. You'll see that it doesn't. This custom of asking "why" is the same as asking which is the most or which is the best. They are very closely related questions that enable you to disconnect yourself from your experience, rather than to identify with it.'

Cage bases his experience on a vision of endless landscape, in which there is room for everything and everyone; it is the American version of pastoral, the world according to nature, in which conflicts are resolved by accommodating them in space. But the most revealing part of Cage's answer is the notion of not interrupting the immersion of ourselves in our experience by asking questions. Particularly, he doesn't want to ask the question of value, because discrimination is possible only by moving out from the level on which we live, the level of process. You can't compare one thing with another while immersed in either. You have to hold them at arm's length, or at mind's length, to judge them at all.

Cage's sentiment is common in criticism of the arts. You find it again in those who propose a theory of performance rather than a theory of knowledge – that artistic excellence is measured by the degree to which a painting or a poem incorporates knowledge about the world. The problem with a theory of knowledge is that it separates subject and object, to begin with, whatever it does thereafter. A theory of performance is best fulfilled in the arts of dance, film, and theatre, and more generally in action and gesture, where there is no separation between subject and object. In dance, we have an art in which 'body is not bruised to pleasure soul'. There is no question of an observing subject separated from what he observes, according to procedures recognised in the theory of perspective and 'point of view'. The revolt against reason, in this context, entails a desire not to observe life but to perform one's own life. The question of self and role-playing remains unanswered, but the art of performance makes available at least a provisional form of unity. The dancer and the dance are one.

The sentiment I'm describing represents a shift in the sense of the arts from meaning to force. Meaning can be given in sentences, it can be translated, it is a companion to reason. But force is not. Force is like the energy of the human body, it is like adrenalin. In the arts, force is inescapably active in the dance, in ballet, which delights in the energy of bodies and the kind of experience it makes possible. Force and mystery are alike because they refuse to identify themselves with reason, but thereafter they differ. Force is the aboriginal power that comes before every show of reason and tries to forestall it. Mystery is what remains after reason, when reason has done its best and its worst; it's what was always there, but unacknowledged, till reason tried to explain it and the explanation, good as far as it went, was puerile thereafter.

The revulsion against reason has rarely been so explicit as in Susan Sontag's essay 'Against Interpretation'. Sontag isn't opposed to interpretation in the Nietzschean sense that everything is interpretation: 'there are no facts, only interpretations.' But she is opposed to the modern style of interpretation in which, as in Freud, a hidden content is to be revealed by dislodging the obvious content. She regards interpretation, in this sense, as yet another example, to use my own terms, of the suppression of force by reason. 'Interpretation', she says, is 'the revenge of the intellect upon art.' By interpreting, we set up a shadow-world of meanings at the expense of the world and its appearances. In the middle of the nineteenth century Henry Adams worried that American intellect wouldn't be able to catch up with American energy: he thought the new forms of energy – dynamos and machinery – wonderful, but they also terrified him: he revered intellect, but couldn't feel sure that the forms it took would be the ones needed in the new circumstances. Sontag has the opposite fear. She is afraid that the intellect has already established a genteel tradition so obtrusive and canonical that energy hasn't a chance. In that sense Sontag is against profundity, which makes a claim upon depth as opposed to surface. What she wants to retain is not depth but intricacy of appearances.

Sontag's theory says 'let it be'.★ As an aesthetic, this has more problems than she has acknowledged. It favours diversity of recognition rather than discrimination. When she prefers one film to another, the reason for the preference is rarely clear: she relies on taste, or a flair she claims for knowing the best. Her attitude is like the one Sir John Pope-Hennessy expresses when he grounds his criticism of art upon connoisseurship. He has spoken of 'the mysterious moment at which intuition becomes belief'. Clearly he means the moment at which *my* intuition becomes *my* belief. But this is just the same as saying 'one is a connoisseur, or one isn't'. And that means putting the mystery where we certainly don't want it to be, in the nature or privileged talent of the critic.

> ★*She calls her programme formalist, but the description is ambiguous. What she has in mind, apparently, is that the most liberating value in art is transparence. 'Transparence means experiencing the luminousness of the thing in itself, of things being what they are.'*

But there is no reason to give up interpreting merely because it is liable to vanity and pretentiousness. To interpret means to make sense or to recover whatever sense the work has made. There is always a temptation, as Wittgenstein said, to try to make the spirit explicit. What we need now is something for which there isn't a precise word; a form of interpretation in which conviction is compatible with the misgiving that should accompany it.§

> §*Misgiving; by which I don't mean 'dawdling', as one reviewer pretended to think.*

Commentary

The problem is: criticism is discursive, but art, when it is most completely art, is not. It may be true that music, painting, and dance attest universal modes of feeling, but the universality that makes words redundant embarrasses criticism. On the level of that universality, there is nothing to be said. Literary criticism is easier in one respect: since literature accommodates discursiveness, there is some degree of continuity between criticism and what it addresses. Problems remain: how to find the right words for processes, forces, actions, gestures, and for appearances that are to be construed as such and not as indications of subterranean truth. Dramatic criticism is more difficult than literary criticism for that reason: discursive language can't easily deal with dynamic processes. But the 'detailed helplessness' of criticism is clearer in, say, music criticism than in literary criticism, because there is, on the level of universality, nothing to be said and yet critics who love music are reluctant to see their loved works fly beyond the reach of syntax. Of course there is much to be said about a piece of music on the technical and analytic level. Leonard B. Meyer's analysis of the Trio of Mozart's G minor Symphony is seventy pages of work closer to the score than any analysis of a poem I have seen. But the gap between that analysis and the universal level of the Trio is what remains to be thought about when the force of the analysis has been registered.

Meyer's analysis is written for musicians and musicologists: the general reader is not intended to read it. A reader who likes music to the extent of 'knowing what he likes' couldn't get beyond Meyer's second page. Criticism addressed to the general listener who is also the general reader is nearly impossible. The gap between music criticism written for such a listener and music criticism written by a musicologist for his colleagues is wider than the corresponding gap in the criticism of literature, theatre, or film. Music suffers particularly from the fact that it doesn't even require the effort of turning over the pages of a book: like a play, a film, or a ballet, it can be enjoyed, on some level, simply by being present. On that level, music is so readily enjoyable that there is little urge to carry the enjoyment further into matters which turn harsh. For that reason, background music is feasible in supermarkets, airports, and living rooms, but background recorded talk would be intolerable: if we heard someone talking, we would want to attend to what he is saying.

Discussions of contemporary music are often confused by forgetting a simple fact. Classical music gives you so much enjoyment that you're rarely impelled to question what it gives or go further in the hope of getting whatever remains. Beyond the point of passivity, it is just as difficult as anything in Schoenberg. Contemporary music gives you so little, so long as your interest remains casual, that only by going further does it become interesting at all. What classical music mostly gives is the security of recognising privileged relations: tonic and dominant; the triad; melody. In the atonal works of Schoenberg, Webern, and Berg, these privileges are withdrawn. The pervasive principle of serial music is permutation of the row: filling all the intervals, lest the listener assume that his traditional right to have his feelings recognised and expressed is still in force. What the common listener values most in traditional music is not his own feelings, given back to him, but the recognition of his privilege in having such feelings.

David Cairns's essay 'How to Enjoy New Music' describes a situation which is generally ignored. Thinking of the common listener, Cairns wonders what such a person makes of the contemporary music he hears. In a fortnight, London audiences heard works by Lutoslawski, Stockhausen, Berio, and Peter Maxwell Davies. What did they make of them? 'We clamour for contemporary music,' Cairns said, 'but when it comes we are apt to be confronted with the awful problem of how on earth to know what we think of it, let alone whether it is any good. What criteria are we to listen to it by?' Cairns doesn't examine a harder question: at what point should criteria be invoked? He assumes that listening and judging are simultaneous, but I would maintain that judging should come later, when all the evidence is in; especially as judging is mostly a matter of comparing one work with another. The trouble with new music and our reception of it is, according to Cairns, that 'you don't even know what you like'.

Cairns first heard Berio's 'Laborintus II' fifteen years ago, and liked it well enough to write enthusiastically about it. But it now seems remote to him. Berio's 'Sinfonia' seems a better work, because the techniques of 'collage, wordless chanting and electronic tape' are 'put to more effective use'. 'But I am forced to recognise that this is a shot in the dark.' Yes, but it is an honest shot. Cairns doesn't say what he means by 'more effective use': it seems to mean 'I like it better' or 'I find it more engaging.' Clearly, 'the gap between creator and critic', so far as Cairns is concerned with 'Laborintus II', has got wider. Cairns doesn't think that, in general, the gap is any wider than it has always been. He refers to the critics who

railed against 'The Rite of Spring' at its first performances. The difference now, he says, is that critics are more careful in what they say. No
critic wants to take the risk of showing himself to be a fool, a few years
after he has denounced a work which eventually gains full acceptance
with audiences. 'Light may sometimes strike.' Lutoslawski's 'Novelette'
now seems 'to make coherent and even quite vivid sense to me', he
reports; but he has heard it several times now at rehearsals and on tape.
'Quite vivid' is a qualifying phrase so strong, however, that the sense the
'Novelette' makes doesn't seem compelling.

With Peter Maxwell Davies's 'Black Pentecost', Cairns's problem is
'how to follow the music: how, on brief acquaintance, to absorb enough
of the musical content to be able to grasp the whole.' The problem is
clear enough in what Cairns says of 'Black Pentecost': virtually nothing,
except that 'the introductory instrumental movement proceeds in a
series of waves, which, together with certain characteristic sea images,
recall the "Second Symphony", that wild paean to the clash of oceans in
the bay below Davies's Orkney home.' The new work 'seemed something of a rehearsal for the symphony, less certain in direction, less
masterful'. But that, Cairns says, 'might have been because I had only
heard it twice'.

I am sure Cairns would be willing to agree that he has nothing useful
to say about 'Black Pentecost'. He doesn't know how the work is
organised. He has no notion of its merit. But none of this is evidence of a
critical disability: he is well qualified, so far as qualifications are in
question, to be a music critic. He has done his homework; listened to
'Black Pentecost' twice, which is twice more than most people's experience and once more than anyone else's, apart from the conductor and the
members of the orchestra. He has read Paul Griffiths's book on Peter
Maxwell Davies, and pondered the composer's advice to deal with his
harmonies by listening to them 'not from the bottom upwards, as
traditionally, but in terms of a tenor, with parts built above and below it,
as happens in mediaeval music'. Easier said than done, as Cairns remarks.

Have his comments on 'Black Pentecost' any value, then? Or are they
totally useless, like Lady Vaizey's comments on Mondrian's painting?
There is a difference. Cairns's few sentences start the process of providing a context for Maxwell Davies's new work: the start is tentative, but
far better than nothing. Several such comments, if the work continues to
be played from time to time, are enough to make the context more stable.
Over a period of years, the work will survive or it won't: much depends

upon the interest conductors take in it, and their authority with orchestras and audiences. The rhetoric of the matter is hard to describe. But a new work by Maxwell Davies needs a context, however tentative; an old work by Mondrian doesn't.

The merit of David Cairns's article is that it doesn't fudge its issue. 'Taking to any composer, but especially a contemporary artist, is often something of an act of faith.' Cairns makes the act in Maxwell Davies's favour. He likes the 'Second Symphony' well enough to trust the composer beyond the audible evidence: if his work includes that symphony, the chances are that the rest of it will be pretty good. But his faith is not a blank cheque; it stops short of 'The Medium', an unaccompanied monodrama written in Maxwell Davies's 'mad' vein for Mary Thomas. This work 'is to me the least interesting part of his output'. Still, 'it is an indisputable *tour de force*.' A very odd thing to say, unless he simply means that he was so overwhelmed by the signs of skill that he couldn't think of anything further or concentrate his mind on the relation between skill and what it served. Peter Maxwell Davies as Paganini? Or was the *tour de force* Mary Thomas's only? Usually we say that something is a *tour de force* when the skill is on display: we would like to have such skill, but we think we'd put it to richer use. You don't know whether or not the work is good, but you couldn't pretend it's not there.

But the phrase keeps us close to the question of helplessness. What can we say, if saying something is called for, about an anxious object? Of course the object is not anxious, but it is such that we, looking at it, feel anxious and project our anxiety upon it. We feel anxious not so much about the status of the object as about our helplessness in its vicinity. It is dismal to feel that our mind is disabled.

One answer is: if you feel anxious, well and good, keep on feeling so, don't indulge yourself in the opportunism of clarity. Anxiety, according to that admonition, corresponds to moral scruple; we may not be clear in the head, but at least we are conscientious. A critic, thus admonished, would accustom himself to living in doubt; either he would assume that at some level of existence everything coheres, or he would postpone indefinitely the question of coherence and live meanwhile with the doubt of appearances. Nothing is worse than premature lucidity, unless it is the satisfaction of enjoying it.

Another answer is provided by the *tour de force*; we think of the work as a purely picturesque event which doesn't call for judgement. Observation is enough. Otherwise put: we think of it by analogy with a force of nature which calls for acknowledgement but not for evaluation. We distance ourselves from the event, and wonder at it. But it is a hard question how long we can continue in that stance. Can we remain in such a relation to the event that it never stops being spectacular, a matter of awe or wonder; or, at some point, are we bound to look for a category, a genre of such events, so that we can release ourselves from it? Much of our understanding is a determination to be done with its object. The normal way of being done with it is to find for it an appropriate slot or bin, even if it is called the sublime or the uncanny. The uncanny is a genre which we maintain by keeping our distance from the object. We know that we don't really dispose of an event by assigning it to a category; it may be different in some way or ways from the other events in the same category. But the mind is assuaged by consigning it to the slot.

Another answer to the anxious object is to engage in its sociology, explaining the larger causes which have issued in this phenomenon. In *Philosophy of Modern Music*, Adorno says that the dissonances which horrify the common listeners to modern music 'testify to their own conditions; for that reason alone do they find them unbearable.' Later he associates Schoenberg's music with shock and trauma: 'passions are no longer simulated, but rather genuine emotions of the unconscious – of shock, of trauma – are registered without disguise through the medium of music.'

Adorno comes to modern music by way of philosophy and sociology. He praises Schoenberg at the expense of Stravinsky, for reasons political and ideological rather than musical. Schoenberg followed his vision of total unity and control in the work of composition; Stravinsky contented himself with pastiche, allusiveness, the backward glance. Schoenberg was truly modern, Stravinsky only speciously so. But Adorno does not extend his political and ideological considerations to the point at which they would be verified (or undermined) by evidence of the ear; presumably because he doesn't trust the common listener's ear enough to appeal to it.

If the bourgeois society is corrupt, our ears have been corrupted, too. No position is secured, then, by claiming, as I would claim, that a good deal of musical criticism is based rather upon the technical interest of the score than upon any evidence of the ear. Matyas Seiber's account of Schoenberg's Third String Quartet emphasises the flexibility of twelve-tone composition. In the first movement the first five notes of the row are used as an *ostinato* in the middle parts, while the remaining seven notes group themselves round them in the phrases of first violin and cello. In the second movement the basic set is distributed among the two violins in two-part harmony, while the viola plays a melody composed of the complete set. In the third movement the theme in the viola presents the basic set, while second violin and cello play the accompaniment in four-note groups, complementing the notes of the viola. In the theme of the last movement, the notes are more freely distributed to emphasise the minor ninth and major seventh intervals.

Seiber has convinced me that the twelve-tone method is indeed flexible, and that 'the number of characters, shapes, textures which can be drawn from the same series is practically limitless.' But I don't see how the question of flexibility or inflexibility can be the crucial question. Seiber hasn't even mentioned the Quartet as one hears it, or the relation between score, performance, and the listener's ear. If he thinks, as Adorno does, that the ear is too corrupted to be invoked, why does he assume that the mind, or whatever faculty deduces evidence of flexibility from the score of the Third String Quartet, is more reliable?

But the most extreme response to the anxious object or the anxiety induced by an indeterminate object is to undermine the discourse which has divided objects into the safe and the dangerous, the known and the indeterminate, the legal and the illegal. Some artists want to maintain the division, but read it mockingly. Francis Bacon has said that he wants to paint the scream rather than the body from which it has issued; presumably because the scream, incorporated in the body, is already on the way to being silenced. He is determined to maintain anxiety by mocking the discourse which offers to allay it. A similar motive is in force in Schoenberg. The old association of dissonance with tension to the degree of pain and of consonance with final resolution and peace is overturned. In the Third Quartet which Seiber has discussed, dissonances are released from their traditional participation in a story of pain and peace; they are allowed to be indifferent. As Adorno remarks of the theme of the slow movement, 'consonances and dissonances stand disinterestedly beside each other: they no longer even sound out of tune.'

The most sustained attack upon a pacifying discourse has come from Foucault. In his early books he thought of discourse as 'merely representation itself represented by verbal signs'. But more recently, concentrating his enquiry upon the relation between knowledge and power, and on the disciplines in which power is exercised, he has started incriminating discourse itself. It now means not merely verbal signs but the whole network of laws, punishments, proscriptions, and conventions by which Western authorities keep themselves in power. In recent essays Foucault has defined humanism as the totality of discourse by which people are controlled and pacified. It is the discourse of humanism that keeps people where they are, allegedly, by forcing upon them a series of subjected sovereignties: 'the soul (ruling the body, but subjected to God); consciousness (sovereign in a context of judgement, but subjected to the necessities of truth); the individual (a titular control of personal rights subjected to the laws of nature and society); basic freedom (sovereign within, but accepting the demands of an outside world and "aligned with destiny").' It follows that discourse tries to rid people of their local anxiety by domesticating its causes.

Foucault's idea is that if you accept the discourse of humanism and the various local discourses which divide experience into safe fields, you are promised a comfortable life within the system. But he hasn't made up his mind about the possibility of defeating the system or inventing some rival forms of discourse. Sometimes he appears to say that resistance to the official discourse would be pointless, since it would merely confirm their mastery and fortify their officers. In those passages he uses the passive rather than the active voice, to say that power is everywhere rather than that anyone in particular exercises it. In other passages he appears to hold that it is possible 'to attack the relationships of power through the notions and institutions that function as their instruments, armature, and armour'.

If we want to translate Foucault's interests into our present terms, the translation would come out somewhat like this. Daily events are anxious objects, worrisome to the officers of humanism because force has appeared without, as yet, the constraint of an official form. But humanism has devised many categories – concepts of man, truth, nature, culture – to dispel the shock of daily occurrences and to neutralise the event. Such categories, being already in place, meet events by insisting on under-standing them; they are already understood, in advance, according to official rhetoric. No event is to be allowed to escape from discourse. Freedom of speech is compatible with humanism because such freedom is constrained by laws and speech itself is 'heard' only within discourse.

What then of the anxious object, as Rosenberg described it, which doesn't know whether it is a masterpiece or junk? Or, extending the description somewhat, what do we say of such objects? First: it is only on occasions of critical discrimination that the question of the status of an anxious object arises. Up to that moment, an object is merely a phenomenon. If it calls for critical judgement, this means that we have reached the point of intending such a judgement. A Foucaultian would have to say that criticism, and especially critical discrimination, is doing society's corrupt work, imposing upon objects a myth of culture, assimilating the new work of art to an accredited system already in place and in force. That is: the critic, according to this rhetoric, treats the anxious object as society treats events, meeting them with humanist categories designed specifically to take the force and the harm out of them. If Rosenberg wants to distinguish an anxious object and determine whether it is a masterpiece or junk, this simply means that he is a humanist, and that he endorses the categories which humanism has devised.

Put like that, Foucault's rhetoric seems libellous, and the seeming is true. He is a moral terrorist: the only question is whether he is willing to throw the bomb or not. If bourgeois humanism were as universally coercive as he maintains, how could he alone have escaped its clutches, or dissociated himself from it in practice? His argument is libellous in many ways, including this one: the categories which bourgeois humanism is supposed to bring to bear upon the shock of daily events – man, culture, nature, truth, and the rest – are not at all as congealed as he maintains. Take, for instance, the idea of culture. Once a normative term, it is now used in a pluralist context, we refer to cultures rather than to Culture. People are almost pedantic in their refusal to prefer one culture to another, and in the respect they offer to customs and conventions other than their own. It is virtually impossible to use the word 'culture' to refer to the possession of distinguished interests or access to the best that has been thought, done, and said in the world. Every term in Foucault's sinister list is similarly malleable: man, nature, truth, self, culture; not one of them has maintained its normative force. Foucault would claim that these categories, if they have been softened in these ways, have yielded to the force of criticism directed upon them by him and other similarly minded writers. No matter: the categories are what they are, not the dread myths Foucault has taken them to be.

My complaint is different. I complain not against bourgeois humanism or even against its discourse, which I regard as flabby rather than coercive; but against the failure of the discourse to allow for occasions on which it might – it should – be driven beyond its common self. I want discourse to allow for the sense in which the only adequate expression is poetry; and the poetry is adequate only insofar as it beckons beyond itself. I refuse to regard that 'beyond' as self-bewilderment or mystification.

But the question then arises: what form should a critical discourse take?

It is encouraging to find in Walter Benjamin, a writer who can hardly be accused of Platonism or of mystification, some notes toward a theory of language which would correspond to an adequate theory of experience. I am referring especially to two essays, a very brief one 'On the Mimetic Faculty' and a longer one 'On Language as Such and on the Language of Man'. It is not necessary for my present purpose to describe these essays in detail: what I value in them is Benjamin's reference to 'the concept that has again and again, as if of its own accord, elevated itself to the centre of linguistic philosophy and constituted its most intimate connection with the philosophy of religion':

This is the concept of revelation. Within all linguistic formation a conflict is waged between what is expressed and expressible and what is inexpressible and unexpressed.

A page or two later Benjamin writes:

The incomparable feature of human language is that its magical community with things is immaterial and purely mental, and the symbol of this is sound. The Bible expresses this symbolic fact when it says that God breathes his breath into man: this is at once life and mind and language.

Benjamin presupposes language 'as an ultimate reality, perceptible only in its manifestation, inexplicable and mystical'.

In quoting these passages I hope, indeed, to make a secularist theory of language less confident of itself, and to discourage its automatic assumption that it always knows what is the case. So I will present the question in another form. What kind of scruple would a critical discourse observe, if it were to respect, rather than ignore, the mystery of the art it addresses?

Wouldn't it, for instance, comport itself in the light of figurativeness as such, respecting the sense of life which finds expression in paradox, metaphor, and tautology? 'I am that I am' is neither nothing nor nonsense. *Occupatio* is a figure, well represented in the rhetoric-books, which refuses to describe and asserts that its powers of description are quite inadequate: 'When he saith something, in saying he cannot say it', as Peacham's *Garden of Eloquence* has it. 'I cannot paint what then I was', Wordsworth says, before he tries to paint it. 'That was a way of putting it – not very satisfactory', Eliot says in 'East Coker'. Even between the modern vernacular languages, some things can't be translated. More generally, there is no good reason to suppose that whatever can be felt can be expressed in words; or indeed in any articulate form.

Another version of critical scruple would arise from consideration of syntax. It is absurd to suppose that the 'juxtaposition without copula' which we find in certain modern poems like *The Waste Land* is nothing but a pretentious claim to profundity; or that a standard syntax could do the job just as well? It seems reasonable to suppose that the procedure corresponds to transitions and dislocations of feeling for which the standard forms of syntax and sequence are definitely not adequate.

I should also mention, and not only because Eliot is never far away from these issues, the matter of incantation. In an early note on Poe and Mallarmé which has been published only in Ramon Fernandez's French translation, Eliot spoke of incantation, as in 'Ulalume' and 'Un Coup de Dés'. Incantation, he said, insists on the primitive power of the Word. He means the Word as such, rather than words used as tokens for something else, their objects of reference. Praising Poe and Mallarmé, Eliot referred to 'la fermeté de leur pas lorsqu'ils passent du monde tangible au monde des fantômes'. He did not spell our that firmness of step, or otherwise gloss the unintimidated sense, in Poe and Mallarmé, of that world of phantoms. He left it to the reader to grasp the relation between the poetic resilience in the poems in question and the power of the Word as such, not at all diminished or humiliated by his calling it primitive.

I will not, I hope, be taken as saying that all poetry should be like Poe's and Mallarmé's, or even that all criticism of the arts should be like Poe's and Mallarmé's criticism of poetry. I am merely bringing forward a few considerations which should, I feel, induce in criticism of the arts a scruple, a sense of the forces engaged in the arts they deal with. If a single phrase were enough, I would recite the passage in 'Notes toward a Supreme Fiction' in which Stevens, with many hints from Valéry, ponders the relation between 'the poet's gibberish' and 'the gibberish of the vulgate'. The gibberish of the vulgate, like that of the Vulgate, is a translation, not an original text; it is gibberish because it desperately tries to say what is adequate and, in the foreseeable failed event, stumbles and splutters. What is common to poet and ordinary man is gibberish, a limping or spluttering translation of a feeling or an intuition we have to think of as aboriginal or otherwise beneath or above our syntax. The poet's gibberish differs from the ordinary man's only as 'the imagination's Latin' differs from – while still being continuous with – 'the lingua franca et jocundissima'.

If something more than a phrase were required, something strong enough to suggest both the mystery of the arts and the misgiving that should accompany whatever we say of them, I would choose a passage from Valéry's *Eupalinos* where, in the dialogue between Socrates and Phaedrus about the arts in general and architecture and music in particular, Socrates says that if an altar were to indicate the diverse character of language, it should have three faces. The first face, almost unformed, would signify the common speech which dies almost as soon as it is born, consumed in its use: it is transformed at once into the bread we have asked for, the road we are shown, the anger of someone who suffers an insult. The second face would pour from its rounded lips a clear fountain of everlasting water – 'jetterait par sa bouche arrondie, un flot cristallin d'eau éternelle' – it would show the noblest traits, eyes large and sublime; the strong, distended neck that sculptures give to the Muses. As for the third face of language: 'Par Apollon, comment figurer celui-ci?' It would be necessary to show some kind of inhuman physiognomy – 'je ne sais quelle physionomie inhumaine' – with those traits of severity and fineness which only the Egyptians have known how to give to the faces of their gods.

What then would misgiving be, in our sense of the arts, if it were not a sense of the three faces of language, and the imagined objects of their gaze?

SIX
A TALENT FOR CONVICTION

The accusations that some modern critics have been making against society amount to this, that it is a liar; it goes out of its way to prevent us from knowing the truth. But I would bring a different charge, that society is guilty of presumption; it presumes to know what reality is, and that it can be fully represented in plain sense and ordinary language without admitting mystery. It assumes that metaphor is only a self-bewildering perversion of a literal truth, and that symbolism is an illicit attempt to endow ordinary things with a radiance which then testifies to their meaning and their value. When I talk about society, I mean such a society as our own, which claims to be free, liberal, and pluralist. The claim is, on the whole, justified, especially if comparisons are made with societies which don't even bother to present themselves as free. But the ideology which makes our society what it is and keeps it in that state has prescribed certain forms of life by representing them as norms: it claims to know the point at which culture may be distinguished from barbarism, and it enforces ways of speaking which make the point of distinction clear. Deviation is permitted only if it is trivial, inept, or otherwise innocuous.

The one risk our society isn't prepared to take is the risk of confessing that it doesn't know what reality is, or what distinguishes fact from illusion. It isn't willing to admit that, as the poet Wallace Stevens said, 'the squirming facts exceed the squamous mind'. A thing is squamous when it consists of thin overlapping parts like the scales of a fish, so a squamous mind is one in which perceptions and axioms are joined together like scales or discs or laminations. If the squirming facts exceed such a mind, it's because they overwhelm its categories. It reminds me of a warning passage in Mann's novel *Dr Faustus* in which the narrator Zeitblom says of liberal theology that while it is an advocate of culture and ready to adapt itself to the ideals of bourgeois society, 'it degrades the religious to a function of the human; the ecstatic and paradoxical elements so essential to the religious genius it waters down to an ethical progressiveness . . . it lacks insight into the daemonic character of human existence.'*

The conventional response to this is that the daemonic character of human existence is merely a vestigial infirmity, that we should have outgrown it and that in any case it can be explained away by psychological discourse. There is a passage in Kenneth Burke's 'Prologue in Heaven', a dialogue between the Lord and Satan, where the Lord tells Satan that mystery is inescapable insofar as temporal, factual knowledge is necessarily fragmentary. But he then says that mystery can be useful in worldly government. 'For, once a believer is brought to accept mysteries, he will be better minded to take orders without question from those persons whom he considers authoritative. So, mysteries are a good grounding for obedience, insofar as the acceptance of a mystery involves a person in the abnegation of his personal judgements.' If we give the argument a further twist, we can say that priests keep the mysteries going to maintain themselves in power; or that artists and critics insist upon the ineffable in art for a similar disgraceful reason, to keep the workers in their lowly place.

But the argument is specious. A good priest doesn't claim to know more than other people; he is a celebrant, not a consultant. He acknowledges mystery, but doesn't claim access to it: his mind is concentrated upon ritual, sacrifice, and the sacraments. Artists and critics shouldn't claim to know mystery, but to be open to its action upon them. Acknowledgement of mystery doesn't mean that we sacrifice our intelligence for some higher cause or that we cultivate the exotic pleasure of believing in something because it's impossible. Wittgenstein put this well by saying that 'what is inexpressible – what I find mysterious and am not able to express – is the background against which whatever I could express has its meaning.'§ I take Wittgenstein's 'whatever I could express' as corresponding to criticism. It is what we can do. But the background is the limit of criticism; we come upon it at the point where words fail. Now the artist is certainly closer to the edge than a critic, closer to the edge of

*Hans Jonas, in a severe but just account of Heidegger's theology, says: 'On pain of immanentism or mere anthropologism, the understanding of God is not to be reduced to the self-understanding of man.' Further: 'The final paradox is better protected by the symbols of myth than by the concepts of thought. Where the mystery is rightfully at home, "we see in a glass darkly." What does "in a glass darkly" mean? In the shapes of myth . . . Myth taken literally is crudest objectification. Myth taken allegorically is sophisticated objectification. Myth taken symbolically is the glass through which we darkly see.'

§Also: 'There are, indeed, things that cannot be put into words. They make themselves manifest. They are what is mystical.' 'Es gibt allerdings Unaussprechliches.

mystery. An artist doesn't know more things or even different things, but he has a special way of knowing what he knows, an unofficial way if the official way is secular and rationalist.★

I think T.S. Eliot spoke well for poetry and the arts when he referred to 'the auditory imagination' and described it as 'the feeling for syllable and rhythm, penetrating far below the conscious levels of thought and feeling, invigorating every word; sinking to the most primitive and forgotten, returning to the origin and bringing something back, seeking the beginning and the end. It works through meanings, certainly, or not without meanings in the ordinary sense, and fuses the old and obliterated and the trite, the current, and the new and surprising, the most ancient and the most civilised mentality.'

We need, then, the variety and latitude of the arts not to provide us with a good choice but to make available the sense of an indefinitely large range of experience other than our own, and of different ways of apprehending it. In theory these acts of imagination should work in us toward livelier sympathies with other people. They may do that in practice. But often they don't. It may happen that the work toward more active sympathy is thwarted in us by more immediate drives and compulsions. We can't safely assume that reading a great novel will do us some kind of good or activate our moral sense. There's no point in being scandalised by reports that commandants in Auschwitz worked all day at their monstrous jobs and went back to their quarters in the evening to listen to Bach or Mozart. There's no scandal. The claims made for the arts, by which they would undertake the duties of priests or otherwise pursue an ethical purpose, are spurious. The relation between the aesthetic sense and the ethical sense it is a matter of speculation; there may be no such relation.§ Or it may be inordinately attenuated by the fact that we conduct our lives on the principle of the division of labour. In any case, reading a good novel won't cure a headache or otherwise improve our temper or disposition.

But it can do one thing; it can enliven in us the sense of the unique presence of objects which come into the

Dies zeigt sich, es ist das Mystische.'

★*Northrop Frye, acknowledging that the development of science has revealed to us richness and variety in the objective world far beyond anything previously known, remarks nonetheless that there is 'a curious restiveness about these disclosures, some feeling of what Blake called "the same dull round, even of a universe".' What is dull, according to Frye, is 'not the universe but the mental operations prescribed for us in observing it'.*

§ *Or if there is, it consists in the ardour and selflessness with which an artist, transcending his appetitive self, shows us — in what he makes, and in the making of it — the world as we would inhabit it if we had*

121

world because artists have created them. While we are aware of these objects, we live for the time being according to a rhythm of interest quite different from our normal rhythm of competition and survival. An *no designs upon it and approached it only with our affection.*

experience is aesthetic when the main quality of it is appreciation, not possessiveness. When we want to possess the object, we have passed into a different sense of it.

But the pleasure of the experience isn't frivolous or casual; it's intelligent pleasure, not only because it arises in the act of consciousness but because one has a complex sense of the relation between the achieved work of art and the factors which go to make its achievement problematic. It's almost a definition of modern art that it is based upon difficulty; not in the sense that every modern work of art is difficult – many of them aren't – but rather that the general context of the arts is of difficulty not local but categorical. Henry James said of Flaubert that 'his case was a doom because he felt of his vocation almost nothing but the difficulty'. The difficulty takes many forms. A poet may feel that the words available to him aren't right, and that they are compromised rather than enriched by the standard wisdom they have been made to serve: that they are 'last year's words'. A composer may feel, as Sir William Walton did, that all the great tunes have been found and used up. A painter may feel that his work is arbitrary, that it has no authority apart from his own assertiveness.

It sometimes appears that modern criticism knows art only as difficulty, and that it has failed to calibrate difficulty, pleasure, and value.* The typical stance of the contemporary critic is one of irony: he is the one who know that we are all bamboozled, he knows the malice of bourgeois ideology, the spuriousness of metaphysics, the idiocy of our desire to ground history upon an intentional origin, whether it is God or a particular concept of man. Indeed, there are two missing factors in contemporary criticism. The first is a set of principles which would renew or establish a sense of value in what we read and look at and hear; which would help us to discriminate between the thousands of objects and events which claim our serious attention. The second is the conviction from which such a set of principles would emerge. Yeats once told Lionel John-

*It is unfortunate that Eliot emphasised 'difficulty' as an almost inevitable mark of modern poetry; as if difficulty were a reliable index of modern spirituality. The rhetoric of Adorno's Philosophy of Modern Music points in the same direction; it amounts to a depreciation of Stravinsky as if he were a mere pasticheur, a charmer, by contrast with Schoenberg, whose music, its

son that he didn't know one member of his generation who practised a talent for conviction. He meant, indeed, religious conviction, and had in view the combined forces of doubt, misgiving, fear, and vacillation which undermine conviction while keeping people in need of it. But if we secularise the phrase a little, we find it applies also to conviction as a force in the criticism of the arts. The only stance to which critics ascribe any point today is that of the ironic, disillusioned observer, observing objects supposed to be ideologically corrupted through and through, and wondering from time to time how he alone has escaped to tell the dismal tidings.

difficulty counting as a virtue, fulfils the moral obligation of being contemporaneous.

More specifically, I'm thinking of the loss of confidence in any assumption of continuity between past and present. Some critics are interested in echoes and allusions between one moment in history and another, but they don't believe that these testify to any large integration. There is a corresponding loss of belief in a relation between form and detail. While we normally assume that the period of Existentialism has ended, it still persists in a common assumption of contingency; that the lived experience is unintelligible, that the detail of life is independent of any form supposedly found in it. Of course we can distance this sense of contingency a little by saying that it is only the perennial problem of finding a relation between fact and value. But the contemporary forms of scepticism are peculiarly dreary, as if they feared that, in a moment's inattention, they would find themselves leaping into faith. Meanwhile the human faculties which are privileged in society are those of measurement and calculation. The pleasure of understanding is explicit in certain currents of criticism from Coleridge to Barthes, but it's still an exotic element in our serious vocabulary.* On the far more casual level of thought represented by writers like Bernard Levin, pleasure is offered as a substitute for understanding, and value as a critical term has virtually disappeared.

*Valéry refers to 'a pleasure which sometimes goes so deep as to make us suppose we have a direct understanding of the object that causes it; a pleasure which arouses the intelligence, defies it, and makes it love its defeat; still more, a pleasure that can stimulate the strange need to produce or reproduce the thing, event, object, or state to which it

There are several ways for critics to set aside the discriminating impulse. They can hand over the entire question to Time, on the easy assumption that Time will make the right decision in each case. Some works of art have survived, so there must have been good reason for their survival. Or the spirit of the age will assert itself and favour those works in which it is embodied. Even when the spirit changes, those works will have entered the history of the arts and will be safe there. The assumption that time will tell is quite reasonable if you are prepared to wait long enough but it consigns us to the infirmity of not knowing what we're doing in the meantime. The critic can say, with the post-Structuralist, that the distinctions between one work and another are of no account compared to the disability they all share; the only difference is *seems attached, and which thus becomes a source of activity* without any definite end, *capable of imposing a discipline, a zeal, a torment on a whole lifetime and of filling it, sometimes to overflowing . . .'* between artists, such as Bataille and Blanchot, who know that their illness is fatal and other artists who don't even know that they are sick. Mostly, though, critics have lost interest in particular works of art except as evidence of a political case to be made and, unfortunately, repeated.

They are only interested in describing the system that makes the production of meanings possible, what Barthes called the empty meaning that sustains all meanings. For such an interest, one work of art is just as good as another. Early Structuralist critics studied the James Bond novels, so that they wouldn't be distracted by questions of quality and value. A critic is, as Donald Davie has well said, 'someone who discriminates among pleasures so as to sharpen them for himself and others.' But there aren't many such around.

These are some of the forces which have diverted criticism of the arts from its proper concern, the discrimination of intelligible pleasures. One of them is especially suggestive, the idea of criticism as writing, an independent activity released from its service to literature and the arts. In practice, such critics rarely separate themselves entirely from the work of art, but their relation to it is loose, they really want to go their own way. 'To move from reading to criticism', Barthes said, 'is to change desires; it is no longer to desire the work but to desire one's own language.' Indeed, much ostensibly theoretic writing in criticism is better understood as autobiography, political rhetoric, or 'musing the obscure'. Once this desire is recognised, the only category to be invoked is taste.

For a long time now it has been impossible to appeal to taste as providing a criterion: taste was in every respect disabled, too subjective, too capricious to be more than personally applicable. It belonged to one's private life. But taste is coming back again, mainly as a patrician attribute which produces its results without the plebeian labour of earning them. In Barthes, for example, criticism became what it has only rarely been, subjective and epicurean. Barthes wanted, especially in his last books, a sensuous relation to phenomena rather than an ethical discrimination of their qualities or consequences. He made room for subjectivity, so long as it was his own. He was not really interested in discriminating between pleasures but in providing more of them, and in showing that it is possible to take diverse pleasure even in a world we are supposedly ready to declare miserable. We can interpret pleasure as a more-or-less continuous satisfaction or, as in Barthes's writing, a momentary bliss: in his case it depends upon a savour, a glance, a phrase. In such epicurean forms it goes with the cult of the fragment, not the large-scale work but the sentence. Style appears as a flicker of eloquence; it accompanies the refusal to be great. Judgement and discrimination are disavowed because they imply an aspiration to completeness which is distasteful to patricians. In judgement and discrimination the detail is chosen only for its representative force and never for the extractable pleasure it provides.

But why am I insisting on judgement and discrimination in our relation to the arts: it can hardly be that the attitude they denote is agreeable? It is a truism that most of our actions are enforced in one degree or another, if only by custom and habit. The aesthetic experience is one of the few in which freedom can still be practised. It is also one of the few on which public or social life does not obtrude. But the main reason for insisting is that our engagement with a work of art is incomplete unless it goes beyond appreciation. I distinguish between aesthetic appreciation and critical discrimination. Appreciation involves absorption in the work, a pause in one's ordinary life to enjoy something other than itself. Discrimination moves the experience beyond itself into a phase of cognition, analysis, and action; it's what R.P. Blackmur meant in saying that critical judgement is 'the last act in bringing particular works of art to full performance'. It is by its culmination in judgement and discrimination that our absorption in the work is brought into the civic context which it shares with other experiences. Without that completion, the experience remains what it was, a pause, time out. The clearest sign of completion is that we are prepared to discuss our principles and discriminations with others.

Kant maintained that a judgement of taste, which says that a work of art is beautiful, makes a proper claim to be universally valid because our satisfaction is purely disinterested, we're not planning to use the work of art. For that reason, a man speaks of the beautiful as if beauty were a quality of the object in question, rather than a mere projection of his own desire for beauty. The conditions under which we discuss such experiences are far harder now than they were in Kant's day: it's hard to have more than a casual conversation touching upon such matters as beauty, form, or taste. These terms are so unfamiliar to us that they cause embarrassment.

But it is too soon to give up the possibility. Speaking of hearing and seeing, Northrop Frye said that 'the word listened to and acted upon is the starting point of a course of action: the visible object brings one to a respectful halt in front of it.' I would hope that the halt in front of the work of art would accept every challenge it offered and acknowledge for all the arts, at the end, what Flannery O'Connor said of fiction, that it is concerned 'with mystery that is lived; ultimate mystery as we find it embodied in the concrete world of sense experience'. And then a talent for conviction brings the experience into the world of speaking and listening.

The best paradigm I can think of for conviction is the speaking of a poem. We normally meet a poem on the printed page, in a book of poems, or a magazine. We read it first with the eye and the mind in conjunction. If we try, we can probably hear some of the phrases, as a musician by looking at a score can hear, at least to some extent, how it goes. But mostly the reading is still silent. Normally we go through the poem, taking it as it seems to want to be taken, stopping if the going gets hard, puzzling it out. Parts of it may be ambiguous. We don't know exactly what goes with what, or where the syntax is taking us. Sometimes it seems simple enough, but there are more choices of meaning than we want. Eliot's 'Whispers of Immortality' begins:

> Webster was much possessed by death
> And saw the skull beneath the skin;
> And breastless creatures under ground
> Leaned backward with a lipless grin.

Was Webster possessed by death as a lover is possessed by his beloved; or as a soul is said to be possessed by a devil; or merely as a scholar or even a seventeenth-century dramatist might be possessed by a theme, held by its possibilities? Are these breastless creatures underground leaning back in a gesture as if sexually compliant, or 'in order to have their laugh out', as William Empson thinks, 'and to look upward at the object of their laughter'? As long as we are reading the poem silently, taking the words on the page, we can mull over these questions and, if we like, leave them undecided.★ But if we read the poem aloud, as I've had to do, we have to settle for one interpretation rather than another. Our voices insist upon speaking with particular emphasis upon some words or syllables rather than others.

Whatever reading you decide on, there is always misgiving; you are aware of the other meanings that are possible. But in a convincing reading you have to convince yourself that one interpretation is, on balance, richer than another. Even then, you have to lean and hearken to the words, trying to catch the sound of their sense. Then the mind settles upon one interpretation, and the voice steadies itself in its favour. This account of how we read a poem is meant to suggest the way in which we should attend to any work of art; entertaining different possibilities but finally committing ourselves to one.

That's a reason why there is no point in comparing the arts with games or even with language-games. A game has rules which the players and spectators accept. If you play soccer or watch a soccer match, you know what constitutes a goal, and how one is scored; you know the off-side rule, and what a foul means. You may not agree with the referee's application of these rules, but that confirms the rules rather than infringing them. If you play chess, you know the rules and fulfil them. In an otherwise uncertain world, games are desirable because they provide the experience of certainty.

★*Empson writes in* Seven Types of Ambiguity: *'Leaned, again, may be verb or participle; either "Webster saw the skull under the skin and the skeletons under the ground, which were leaning backwards" (leaned may be a verb with "that" understood, as so often in English, but it is hard to distinguish this case from the participle), or, stressing the semi-colon, "Webster saw the skull under the skin, but meanwhile, independently of him, and whether seen or no, the creatures underground leaned backward", both in order to have their laugh out, and to look upward at the object of their laughter. The verse, whose point is the knowledge of what is beyond knowledge, is made much more eerie by this slight doubt.'*

The only certainty in the arts is that everything that happens in them is in parentheses. In *La Bohème* Mimi dies only in brackets; it is all 'as if' she died. We know this, but Rodolfo doesn't, because he, too, lives in parentheses. This is different, though not totally different, from a hypothetical situation that might be offered, conversationally, for our judgement. Just suppose that such and such were to happen. In the play or the opera, the feelings are so presented that we take them as if they were real, while also knowing that they are imaginary. In New York a few years ago, I saw, in the Whitney Gallery, a sculpture of a foot-sore woman resting herself heavily on a chair just inside the door. The work was so extraordinarily realistic that I didn't know, and for quite a while couldn't decide, whether it was a sculpture or a real foot-sore woman.* This was unsettling, because part of an aesthetic experience is knowing that it is one, that the parentheses of form are in place. We have to know that we are dealing with imaginary objects, even while we're responding to them as if they were real.

*It turned out to be Duane Hanson's 'Woman with Dog' (1977). I forgot the dog.

The poet Marianne Moore had something like this in mind when she said that poets should present 'imaginary gardens with real toads in them'. The gardens are imaginary, but I wouldn't want to associate them too easily with the processes of fantasy and day-dreaming. Neither fantasy nor day-dreaming will ever produce a work of art. The imaginary objects of art are not pretences, they are proposed as not being real, but their relation to the real may be one of likeness or difference in nearly any degree.

The same equivocal character obtains in judging the arts. The judgements we make of them have the advantage of being disinterested, because the fact that their objects are imaginary removes them from our ordinary needs and desires. But this disinterestedness is challenged at every point, as in *King Lear* or *La Bohème*, by sympathies and revulsions which nearly break through the conventions by which the artistic events appear at all. It is easier to declare an object as imaginary than to feel an emotion as imaginary. So our judgements of a work of art are different, though not totally different, from those we make in ordinary life, where the parentheses are removed and we judge in terms of local interests and needs. The arts are at once real and unreal; and, in responding to them, we are at once detached and involved. Their significance, the way in which they become present to us, arises from that strange set of conditions.

There's a corresponding doubleness in the way we value the arts. In one sense they are trivial. If you're hungry or in pain, no work of art will help you; though, when the pain is over, a poem or a symphony may help to express what you feel. When Emily Dickinson writes, 'After great pain a formal feeling comes', you may know the formality, that stiffness or congealment, better for her saying it. But while you're in pain, the poem is no help. Robert Frost said that the theme of poetry is 'how to surmount the pressure upon us of the material world'. But if the pressure is acute or painful, poetry is helpless. I want to put the case differently. Let's concede that in one way the arts are useless: they won't cure a toothache. But in another way they are really momentous, because they provide for spaces in which we can live in total freedom. Think of it as a page. The main text is central, it is the text of need, of food and shelter, of daily preoccupations and jobs, keeping things going. This text is negotiated mostly by convention, routine, habit, duty, we have very little choice in it. So long as we are in this text, we merely coincide with our ordinary selves. If the entire page were taken up with the text, we would have to live according to its conventional rhythms, even in our leisure hours; because those, too, are subjected to conventions.

The arts are on the margin, and it doesn't bother me to say that they are marginal. What bothers me is the absurd claims we make for them. I want to say that the margin is the place for those feelings and intuitions which daily life doesn't have a place for, and mostly seems to suppress. And the most important intuition is of mystery as what Eliot called 'the ground of our beseeching'. Even in a world mostly secular, the arts can make a space for our intuition of mystery, which isn't at all the same thing as saying that the arts are a substitute for religion. There is nothing in art or in our sense of art which corresponds to my belief in God. In religion, our faith and love are directed beyond ourselves. In art, faith doesn't arise. It's enough that the arts have a special care for those feelings and intuitions which otherwise are crowded out in our works and days. With the arts, people can make a space for themselves, and fill it with intimations of freedom and presence.

Commentary

I got into trouble with Melvyn Bragg for saying that the arts are marginal. On the *Voices* programme he said:

> He declares that in his opinion the Arts are marginal, and he cuts them off from religion. As far as I'm concerned, the Arts are not marginal, and as far as I'm concerned, you can't cut them off from reactions which share in the religious experience. The Arts can be central and they can be vital.

But the passage in this last lecture which gave most offence came at the end, where I said:

> Even in a world mostly secular, the arts can make a space for our intuition of mystery, which isn't at all the same thing as saying that the arts are a substitute for religion. There is nothing in art or in our sense of art which corresponds to my belief in God. In religion, our faith and love are directed beyond ourselves. In art, faith doesn't arise.

On the *Voices* programme the chairman Robert Hutchison took this to mean 'that religion can't be assimilated to art, and art can't be assimilated to religion'. I wasn't sure what that, in turn, meant, so I tried to make a distinction, roughly on these lines.

Suppose I said: 'I believe in God.' Suppose I emphasised the verb even more than its object. Belief, with that emphasis in mind, doesn't arise in the aesthetic experience. The formal parentheses are always in place; it's always 'as if' something were the case. Suppose now that, instead of 'God', I referred to 'the gods'. If I were talking about Greek tragedy, for instance, I would have to refer to the gods, and try to imagine what sense of life the gods provoked for the Greeks. I don't believe in the gods in anything like the sense in which, as a Roman Catholic, I believe in God. But in the aesthetic experience I want to retain something of the Eleusinian sense which was once provoked by the gods; or something of the sense of mystery which a reference to the gods might evoke, even today. I want to keep in mind the fictiveness of art, and at the same time acknowledge the seriousness which fictiveness does not in any way refute.

Well, all I got for taking the pains of this distinction was a review by Peter Kemp in *The Times Literary Supplement* entitled 'The Theology behind the Theorizing'. Kemp evidently finds it impossible to imagine what a religious belief might be; or any process which might lead to religious conviction. Reading his review, I was reminded of F.R. Leavis's great phrase, 'the darkness of enlightened men'. Kemp referred to 'the frozen facial expressions' my allusion to 'the gods' produced in my colleagues. Eagleton, according to Kemp, 'pounced on the hieratic imagery as overt evidence of the theology behind the theorizing': he saw me in my 'crypto-theological corner'.

'Crypto-', added to a word, means 'concealed, unavowed'; in this case, I report that my theology is that of Catholicism (Roman), a fact I am not conscious of having concealed. Terry Eagleton is well aware of my position; he had no need to pounce on my hieratic imagery to find evidence of my theology. But in any case: is assent to Catholic theology a crime in England again, as it once was? Is it especially scandalous to English ears, as indeed for centuries it was, that Catholic theology is audible in an Irishman? I confess I am a little surprised that a set of lectures featuring, from time to time, such words as mystery, presence, and 'the gods' should have defeated not only Peter Kemp's goodwill but, a more telling consideration, his imagination.

I am very unwilling to end on this surly note or – what amounts to the same thing – to yield my context to the dreary secularism Peter Kemp may be taken, for the moment only, to represent.

Sometime before I wrote the Reith Lectures, I published in *Sewanee Review* an essay 'On the Limits of a Language'. It now seems to me to represent some of the considerations, mostly about language, from which the' Lectures emerged. I take the liberty of printing it here, mainly in the hope that it may restore the Lectures to the setting and tone in which they began.

It is prudent to speak to a text, and it may be wise to keep at hand a passage from the first canto of the *Paradiso* in which Dante, gazing upon Beatrice who is gazing upon the sun, speaks of an experience which lies beyond nature and in the same breath says that it is impossible to speak of such a thing: 'Trasumanar significar per verba/non si poría.' ('The passing beyond humanity may not be set forth in words.') We speak of such experiences, but vainly: we know we cannot translate or express them. It is reasonable to assume that there are experiences which lie so far beyond 'nature' – however we elucidate that word – that words have never been found for them, and will never be found. It is also reasonable to make the same assumption of experiences which lie beneath nature. It is impertinent to assume that there are words for every experience; if there were, music, sculpture, and silence would be redundant. I find it congenial to believe that there are moments at which language stands baffled, saying of what it has just said that that is not it at all, not at all. Such moments are congenial because they tell against the idolatory of language to which we are all, in some of our moods, susceptible. Knowing that language has done so much, we want to believe that it can do everything.

Idolatry of language marks an outer limit of my theme. The theme itself can take a more palpable form if we agree to think not chiefly of Language as such but of particular languages, resorting to the lower case. I refer to the situation in which a writer using a particular language feels that he has reached a limit either of that language or of his own sense of it. He has made raids on the inarticulate and returned with nothing to show for his labour. Is there not a recognition of this kind in the *Paradiso* when Dante says that it is impossible to signify in words the experience of transcending the human state and, as if to mime the impossibility, swerves from his otherwise capable vernacular into a Latin more erudite in its sense of that experience? Dante is referring to St Paul's experience as reported, however inadequately, in Second Corinthians, how a man in Christ 'was caught up into paradise and heard unspeakable words, which it is not lawful for a man to utter'. Paul does not know whether the man caught up into paradise retained his bodily nature or transcended it in a spiritual nature. He doesn't know whether he was in or out of his body. Dante feels the same bewilderment in gazing upon Beatrice, and he invokes in the *per verba* not only the episode in Corinthians but the tradition in which its meaning has most been pondered, the Latin tradition notably of Augustine and Aquinas, Dante's chief instructors on the relation between human experience and that outer limit of it which testifies, however inadequately, to a vision of God. In the letter to Can Grande della Scala, Dante refers to the same passage of Corinthians and draws from it the same lesson; that the human mind may reach such a state of ecstasy that, after it returns to its normal condition, memory fails, since it has transcended the range of human faculty: *propter transcendisse humanun modum*. The same lesson is recited from Matthew and from

Ezekiel. Dante goes on to say in the letter that we perceive many things by the intellect for which language has no words – 'a fact which Plato indicates plainly enough in his books by his employment of metaphors, for he perceived many things by the light of the intellect which his everyday language (*sermone proprio*) was incapable of expressing.'

These questions are pondered in Latin because Latin is wiser than the vernacular languages in the understanding of spiritual experiences. It may be suggested that the point is invalidated by the *De Vulgari Eloquentiae*, in which Dante seems to say that the vernacular language is older than Latin and more intimately related to the original experience of God's presence. Dante's notion is that Adam's language was Hebrew and that the modern European languages emerged from Hebrew as three great linguistic families. Latin, according to this notion, was an artificial language, deliberately constructed in conventional changeless terms so that our knowledge of distant times and peoples would be preserved. It was never a native or mother language. But the point is not invalidated. Apart from the fact that Dante's ideas on the origin of languages, as outlined in the *De Vulgari Eloquentiae*, are virtually renounced in *The Divine Comedy*, there is a clear recognition that Latin, whether older or younger than the vernacular languages, is the language in which the question of the relation between experience and speech has been most fully pondered and debated. The stability of Latin, especially the Latin of Augustine and Aquinas, is invoked in debating such questions as the speech of God, the original language of Adam, the building of Babel, the confusion of tongues. The *De Vulgari Eloquentiae* is itself written in Latin, although its major theme is a description of an ideal vernacular language. In the passage from the *Paradiso* Dante is pointing toward a mode of experience for which an impossibly pure and rarefied language would be required, the speech of angels; and we are to imagine not the thing itself but its possibility and then its absence from vernacular expression. (Later: I note that Frye says, in *The Great Code*, 'perhaps it is only through the study of works of human imagination that we can make any real contact with the level of vision beyond faith. For such vision is, among other things, the quality in all serious religions that enables them to be associated with human products of culture and imagination, where the limit is the conceivable and not the actual.') The effect of the Latin is to lead the mind beyond its vernacular concerns toward a language neither Latin nor Italian but the original language before Babel, in which, we assume, anything that could be experienced could be expressed.

This runs beyond my theme. I am concerned with the situation in which a poet, let us say, writing his poem in one language swerves into another. I am not satisfied with the explanation that a poet with a mind well stocked in several languages is mere taking the satisfaction of disclosing his possessions. It is sometimes maintained of *The Waste Land* that a poem proceeding by association and contrast naturally issues in the linguistic diversity with which the poem ends, and that it is a sufficient explanation that the poet wanted to transcend the limits of any single language. I am not persuaded. Eliot was remarkably sensitive not only to associations and contrasts but to the transitions from one tone to another. His imagination, like his theology, was responsive to different levels of being, and to the fact that only a critical analysis establishes at any moment what the particular level is. In 'Poetry and Drama' he said that 'a mixture of prose and verse in the same play is generally to be avoided: each transition makes the auditor aware, with a jolt, of the medium.' Such a mixture is justified 'when the author wishes to produce this jolt: when, that is, he wishes to transport the audience violently from one plane of reality to another.' The jolt which takes place when a dramatist changes from prose to verse in the same play can be produced by other means: it is much the same as the jolt we feel when two different dictions are brought together, as in Emily Dickinson's phrase 'a quartz contentment'.

I am thinking, more particularly, of the several languages in Pound's *Cantos*, and of such moments as the flurry of Provençal at the end of Dante's *Purgatorio* 26 and the 'Raphel' line in *Inferno* 31. Scholars say that the 'Raphel' line is meant as gibberish, not in Wallace Stevens's sense of 'the poet's gibberish' but a more abysmal or demotic sense; more like *King Lear*'s 'matter and impertinency mixed, reason in madness'. These occasions are difficult to compare. The Provençal lines ascribed to Arnaut Daniel though composed by Dante are a supreme compliment by which one master allows another to speak in his own tongue rather than suffer the indignity of a swift transition into modern Italian. As for the single line permitted to Nimrod before he is suppressed: he is his own accuser, Dante's Italian says ('Elli stessi s'accusa'), presumably because he tries to communicate in his own tongue and finds it impossible because of the gross confusion of tongues he caused at Babel. Whatever Nimrod's words mean to him, there is no evidence that they intend self-accusation. The linguist ('per lo cui mal coto / pur un linguaggio nel mondo non s'usa' – 'through whose ill thought one language only is not used in the world') could offer a justification of his actions by appealing to an extreme nationalism of sentiment: the fact that the appeal would be incommunicable would point not to a defect in his programme or even to an error of method but merely to consequences beyond his intention. It is charming that Dante's Virgil rounds upon Nimrod and rebukes him in strict Italian, a language which by definition Nimrod can't understand any better than Virgil can understand Nimrod's idiolect, though I assume that the gestures of anger make a universal language understandable by anyone. We can all understand a fury in the words, if not the words.

We often neglect this form of understanding; we are so concerned to link words to understanding and understanding to words that we disable ourselves in receiving signs which come before, after, or beneath words; or in acknowledging manifestations which are not signs at all. Virgil is not a patient critic, though his morality is impressive; he should have attended to the fury in Nimrod's words, if it is fury, and not to the words. By patience I mean the attitude William Carlos Williams displayed when he met in Pound's early cantos fragments of foreign languages he couldn't read: 'As to the Greek quotations – knowing no Greek – I presume they mean something, probably something pertinent to the text – and that the author knows what they mean. . . . In all salient places, Pound has clarified his outland insertions with reasonable consistency. They are no particular matter save that they say, there were other times like ours – at the back of it all.' This is incomplete, but not entirely inadequate. A scholar knows that the outland things in the *Cantos* are particular matter and that many of them say that there have been other times different from ours and better. But Williams's patience, his assent to the otherness of perception, is the right start for any further recognitions. Williams respects the foreign elements in Pound's poem as testifying to feelings and recognitions which Pound wanted to keep in a somewhat foreign state rather than have them assimilated too easily to his sensibility. Even a reader of Greek will keep the Greek bits in his mind, undomesticated. It is a mark of Pound's imagination, more than of Eliot's in *The Waste Land* and the early poems generally, that the foreign elements are allowed to hold themselves intact, and distant. I shall argue later, however, that the relation between Eliot and Dante makes a crucial exception to this general rule.

There are many possible reasons to account for a poet's recourse to elements outside his own language. He may think that the particular feeling in the case is not fully expressed, or even well expressed, in the native language. In 'Fragment of an Analysis of a Case of Hysteria' Freud breaks into French when he wants to invoke an attitude of intelligent worldliness in sexual matters. They order these things better in French. Luther's table-talk shows that he switched from German to Latin when the theme became intellectual or, more especially, theological. Again a writer may feel that another language has developed more adequately the expression of a particular range of experience. No modern language is as good as Dante's Italian for practising the imagery of light, of spiritual vision, radiance of being.

There may also be disciplines enforced more completely in one language than another. When the 'familiar compound ghost' of Eliot's 'Little Gidding' says,

> From wrong to wrong the exasperated spirit
> Proceeds, unless restored by that refining fire
> Where you must move in measure, like a dancer,

it is a bonus for the reader if he recalls the refining fire of Purgatorio 26, 'Poi s'ascose nel foco che li affina' ('Then he hid himself in the fire that purifies them'), the line used again at the end of *The Waste Land*. But it is merely a bonus, a good reader manages well enough without it. But Eliot could not manage without a quality in Dante which he lacked in his own talent. It was not even a matter of talent, but of spiritual disposition. The point is sufficiently made by remarking the idealist character of Eliot's genius – Hugh Kenner has referred to Eliot's Symbolism as a procedure for signifying ineffabilities – and the limitation of sympathy that goes with it, the obstacles he had to surmount within himself before he could acknowledge motives radically different from his own. F.H. Bradley's philosophy merely confirmed a sense of the inevitable imprisonment of self which was congenital in Eliot. A.C. Charity has argued most persuasively that Eliot has recourse to Dante 'whenever an encounter with an "other" is required by pressure of an urgently confessional horror'.

It is generally agreed that the unequivocal acknowledgement of feelings separate from his own and equal to his own in the degree of their force came hard to Eliot. His plays were important to him if only as exercises in that acknowledgement. In Eliot's poetry objects tend to lose their identities and to become functions of the subject – a tendency not at all countered by Eliot's insistence, in theory, upon the impersonality of art. Dante was necessary to Eliot because of Dante's uncompromised recognitions: his poetry provoked Eliot to go beyond the limits of his temper and to believe in the reality of other people. Sometimes, as in the refining fire of 'Little Gidding', it was enough merely to allude to Dante: enough, so that Eliot could engage in the spiritual exercise of recalling the force of Dante's acknowledgements. But in a mere allusion, as in a translation of Dante's Italian into Eliot's English, there was always a danger of staining the translation with Eliot's own subjectivity, or of making Dante dance to Eliot's quite different measure. There were occasions, as in the 'Sovegna vos' of 'Ash-Wednesday', when nothing less than Dante's Italian would suffice. It is impossible to assimilate another's feeling completely to your own, or dissolve it in your subjectivity, if you allude to it in a foreign language and place it beside the domestic version of your own.

Eliot did not need Dante's authority to justify his own feelings. His poetry is uncompromising in its commitment to the kind of memories, images, and associations he referred to in the 'Conclusion' to *The Use of Poetry and the Use of Criticism*:

Why, for all of us, out of all that we have heard, seen, felt, in a lifetime, do certain images recur, charged with emotion, rather than others? The song of one bird, the leap of one fish, at a particular place and time, the scent of one flower, an old woman on a German mountain path, six ruffians seen through an open window playing cards at night at a small French railway junction where there was a watermill: such memories may have symbolic value, but of what we cannot tell, for they come to represent the depths of feeling into which we cannot peer.

He needed Dante when he felt called upon, as by a scruple, to recognise other feelings beyond the spreading stain of his own.

It is sometimes maintained that the recognition of feelings other than one's own is a mark of civility, and that many people can't rise to it. Barthes has argued in *Mythologies* that 'the petit-bourgeois is a man unable to imagine the Other':

If he comes face to face with him, he blinds himself, ignores and denies him, or else transforms him into himself. In the petit-bourgeois universe all the experiences of confrontation are reverberating, any otherness is reduced to sameness.

I can't believe that the other social classes would escape whipping if this criterion were applied to them: peasants, factory-workers, and aristocrats are not distinguished by their capacity for imagining or acknowledging the Other. But we may let the point lapse. The rebuke may be retained by ascribing it not to a social class but to any failure of the imagination: we call it egotism.

When Eliot discussed these questions, he used an entirely different idiom. He spoke of Tradition rather than of Otherness. But in any case he was himself the first person he needed to convince. It is only by an immense effort of conscientiousness that a poet as subjective as Eliot can turn toward the diverse recognitions which constitute a tradition in Eliot's sense. That he made such an effort is clear: it corresponds in aesthetic terms to the process which resulted in his conversion to Anglicanism. But it went against his grain, and that is its chief interest. The fragments shored against the narrator's ruins at the end of *The Waste Land* are given in their own languages not merely as selected constituents of Tradition expressing themselves as if in different voices, but as voices testifying to Otherness. It is not merely that 'shantih' would be inadequately represented by 'the peace that passeth understanding', but that such peace is already too completely domesticated: it is a platitude of Christendom and therefore too close to our common selves, even if we are not Christians. It is quite possible to be irritated by these foreign bits, and to complain of them, as Graham Hough does in his *Image and Experience* because of 'the hideously awkward gear-change, the intrusion of an alien rhythm and an alien vowel-system, into verse otherwise distinguished by the fineness of its auditory imagination'. (Later: That last phrase – the auditory imagination – which I quoted from Eliot in the sixth lecture, suggests that the 'feeling for syllable and rhythm, penetrating far below the conscious levels of thought and feeling' to which he refers would find fulfilment in a wider linguistic range than that of a single language.) But the alien quality of the rhythm and vowel-system is what Eliot wanted of the foreign bits; their intrusiveness is their virtue, the linguistic form of otherness.

There are two situations to be reckoned with, even if one is only an extreme form of the other. In the first, the English or American poet takes over the foreign lines and keeps them untranslated, as at the end of *The Waste Land*. In such cases, nothing less than the full testament of otherness will do. The poet has reached a limit of some kind in his relation to the native language. In the second situation, the poet alludes to an earlier poem, either by translating it into his English or by invoking its motif in some other way. This second situation would not show the degree of perturbation or of conscientious effort evident in the first; but it would still suggest a limit or a crisis. I am referring to the movement of feeling which can be appeased only by resorting to the different tradition of another language. Sometimes the degree of crisis is clear in the form the translation takes. At the end of 'Little Gidding' Eliot writes:

And all shall be well and
All manner of thing shall be well
When the tongues of flame are in-folded
Into the crowned knot of fire
And the fire and the rose are one.

This is English written with the formal gravity of a mind attentive to the English translations of the Bible; there is also a recollection of a passage from the *Shewings* of Juliana of Norwich. But the fire and the rose come as motifs from Dante, and the in-folding of the tongues of flame. *In-folded* draws particular attention to itself not only because of its position at the end of the line but because, in its given form, it has only marginal existence in English. Normally it is taken as an obsolete variant of 'enfolded', and while it has a frail claim to separate existence it can't be said to be at home in the language. It appears to mark the point, therefore, at which the relation between Eliot's language and Dante's becomes problematic. I assume it comes from the passage in *Paradiso* 33 which Eliot quoted in the major essay on Dante:

Nel suo profundo vidi che s'interna,
    legato con amore in un volume,
        ciò che per l'universo si squaderna.

('In its depth I saw ingathered, bound by love in a single volume, that which is dispersed in leaves through the universe.') *Ingathered* is the word given in the translation Eliot quotes, a slightly modified version of Philip Wicksteed's translation in the old Temple Classics. When it becomes *in-folded* it holds itself aloof from the language surrounding it: the relation between *in-folded* and the general body of the English language is quite different from the relation between 's'interna' and the general body of Dante's Italian. It may be said that this proves the translation defective, on the ground that a common phrase in one language shouldn't be translated by a rare phrase in the other. This might hold in a case like that of the first lines of *Paradiso* 28, in which 'Quella che imparadisa la mia mente' is regularly Englished as 'she who imparadises my mind'. English is weak in these enfolding verbs, Italian is strong in them. In the passage from 'Little Gidding' Eliot seems determined to rise to Dante's occasion, even at the cost of using a rare English word and causing a flurry in the passage as a result.

He has something different in view in *The Waste Land*:

> Unreal City,
> Under the brown fog of a winter dawn,
> A crowd flowed over London Bridge, so many,
> I had not thought death had undone so many.
> Sighs, short and infrequent, were exhaled,
> And each man fixed his eyes before his feet.

'Unreal' reverberates through the poem, as if provoked by 'undone': a quality dissolved, an action retracted. Eliot once said that Baudelaire's lines about the 'Fourmillante Cité' – in 'Les Sept Vieillards' – summed up for him the entire significance of that poet. I think Baudelaire's adjective accounts for one of the puzzling features of Eliot's lines, the fact that the singular noun *crowd* is given a plural adjective, *so many*. We would expect a crowd to be qualified as vast, enormous, or some such, but Eliot turns it at once into multiplicity by straining the grammar. I think he has in mind not only Dante's crowd in *Inferno* but the swarming city, multiple, each man dreaming his own dream, meeting his own spectre, which is Baudelaire's city. In the corresponding passage in *Inferno* 3 Dante emphasises in 'sì lunga tratta / di gente' ('so long a train of people') the collective nature of the crowd, not the individual cowards but cowardice itself, souls collectively lost. 'I had not thought death had undone so many': a motif of extraordinary salience in Eliot's entire work, the configuration in which action is confounded or undermined. In relation to Eliot and Dante it goes all the way from La Pia's line at the end of *Purgatorio* 5, 'Siena mi fé, disfecemi Maremma' ('Siena made me, Maremma unmade me') to the allusion in *The Waste Land*,

> Highbury bore me. Richmond and Kew
> Undid me;

and it includes lines from Thomas Heywood which Eliot quoted in his essay on that dramatist as lines which 'no men or women past their youth can read without a twinge of personal feeling':

O God! O God! that it were possible
To undo things done; to call back yesterday.

Thus far, Eliot has been alluding to Dante and Baudelaire, according to a procedure he described – in 'What Dante Means to Me' – as an attempt 'to arouse in the reader's mind the memory of some Dantesque scene, and thus establish a relationship between the medieval inferno and modern life'. He goes on:

> Readers of my *Waste Land* will perhaps remember that the vision of my city clerks trooping over London Bridge from the railway station to their offices evoked the reflection 'I had not thought death had undone so many'; and that in another place I deliberately modified a line of Dante by altering it – 'sighs, short and infrequent, were exhaled.' And I gave the references in my notes, in order to make the reader who recognised the allusion know that I meant him to recognise it, and know that he would have missed the point if he did not recognise it.

The source of the line is *Inferno* 4:

> Quivi, secondo che per ascoltare,
>   non avea pianto mai che di sospiri
>   che l'aura etterna facevan tremare

– Dante's description of Limbus, the first circle of Hell, inhabited by the souls of virtuous pagans, the unbaptised who live in darkness, longing, and hopelessness: 'Here there was no plaint, that could be heard, except of sighs, which caused the eternal air to tremble.' The preceding line in Eliot translates Dante, but this one veers from him. Presumably the point we are to take care not to miss in the alteration is that while the passive voice makes the sighs abstract, the adjectives 'short and infrequent' give them the mechanical quality of beings neither alive nor dead:

> Sighs, short and infrequent, were exhaled,
> And each man fixed his eyes before his feet.

In Dante the sighs are generic and congenital; in Eliot, mechanical. In the first line Eliot goes to Dante as pupil goes to master; in the second, he swerves from him. Eliot spoke of the poet's obligation 'to explore, to find words for the inarticulate, to capture those feelings which people can hardly even feel, because they have no words for them'. Eliot's feelings are his own, but the words for them are often Dante's; when they are, they challenge Eliot – the challenge being, indeed, always accepted – not only to express his feelings as if he were convinced of them but to criticise them, rebuke them, and call forth other feelings to complete them, feelings which we may assume he could not even feel without the alien words. The process is akin to the one Yeats had in view when, in *A Vision*, he spoke of holding in a single thought reality and justice. Justice is what we are not obliged to hold in our thought, and what we would not think of holding if we were fully satisfied – morally satisfied with the 'reality' of our feelings; it is what I mean by referring to scruple, which is the sense of justice in practice.

But what does it signify, when a line in Eliot alludes to something in Dante or Baudelaire? Is it merely a reflection of the fact that nothing has its meaning by itself, but must be completed – or at least extended in its bearing – by having its relation to other things indicated? I am thinking of two versions of this extension. The first is Philip Wheelwright's description of the archetypal imagination, 'which sees the particular object in the light of a larger conception or of a higher concern'. The second is René Girard's definition of the chivalric relation between Don Quixote and Amadis of Gaul. 'Chivalric existence is the *imitation* of Amadis in the same sense that the Christian's existence is the imitation of Christ.' And later: 'Chivalric passion defines a desire *according to Another*, opposed to the desire *according to Oneself* that most of us pride ourselves on enjoying.' In either of these versions, the poetic imagination disavows any claims we are inclined to make for our words, or for the knowledge we enforce in them. The true meaning is elsewhere, it does not inhere in the object or in our asserted possession of it. The proper sense of words is not in their particular claim to mean and to control the object of their attention; it is to be apprehended, rather, from the relation between the words and the silence that surrounds them.

(Later: There are silences and silences. 'Whereof one may not speak, thereof one must be silent.' There is the silence of bewilderment, in which something we have taken as a problem has defeated us. That's not the silence I have in mind. If you can pluck out the heart of a mystery, it was not a mystery in the first place. The proper form of silence is like the relation between something we say and the misgiving with which we say it, knowing how partial or otherwise inadequate it is. Or like the relation between faith and the doubt that is inseparable from it. We're more likely to feel this relation between speech and silence when we've listened to a piece of music or looked at a sculpture or a painting than when we've read a novel or a poem. Because novels and poems are words, we tend to think they're susceptible to our words: as they are, indeed, but only up to a point.)

BIBLIOGRAPHY

INTRODUCTION

St Augustine, *The City of God*, XII, 18 (Migne, *Patrologia Latina*, XLI, p.368); and *On Christian Doctrine*, I, 6 (Migne, *PL* XXXIV, p.21)
E.M. Cioran, *La Tentation d'Exister* (1956): *The Temptation to Exist*, tr. Richard Howard (Chicago: Quadrangle Books, 1968, p.152)

LECTURE ONE

Walter Benjamin, *Reflections*, ed. Peter Demetz (New York: Harcourt Brace Jovanovich, 1978, pp.178–179, 191)
R.P. Blackmur, *Form and Value in Modern Poetry* (New York: Doubleday, 1957, pp.121–122). *The Lion and the Honeycomb* (London: Methuen, 1956, p.41)
Kenneth Burke, *Counter-statement* (1931:1953) (Los Altos: Hermes Publications, 1953, p.119). *A Grammar of Motives* (1945:1955) (New York: Braziller, 1955, p.219)
John Cage, *M: Writings 67–72* (London: Calder and Boyars, 1973, p.xi)
Gilles Deleuze, *Proust et les signes* (1964): *Proust and Signs*, tr. Richard Howard (London: Allen Lane, 1973, pp.40–41)
John Dewey, *Art as Experience* (New York: Minton, Balch, 1934, p.7)
T.S. Eliot, *The Use of Poetry and the Use of Criticism* (London: Faber and Faber, 1933, p.111)
Henry James, *The Tragic Muse* (1890) (London: Rupert Hart-Davis, 1948 reprint of first edition, p.487). *The Art of the Novel: Critical Prefaces*, with an Introduction by R.P. Blackmur (New York: Scribner's, 1934, p.79)
André Malraux, *The Voices of Silence* (1953), tr. Stuart Gilbert (Princeton: Princeton University Press, 1978 reprint, p.639)
Gabriel Marcel, *Être et Avoir* (1935), *Being and Having*, tr. Katharine Farrer (Westminster: Dacre Press, 1949, pp.100–101)

145

Ezra Pound, 'Hugh Selwyn Mauberley' (1920): *Selected Poems* (New York: New Directions, 1957, p.61)

Charles S. Peirce, *Values in a Universe of Chance*, ed. Philip P. Wiener (New York: Doubleday, 1958, p.406)

John Crowe Ransom, *The World's Body* (1938:1968) (Baton Rouge: Louisiana State University Press, 1968, p.42)

Harold Rosenberg, *The De-definition of Art* (London: Secker and Warburg, 1972, p.218)

George Santayana, *Three Philosophical Poets* (Cambridge, Mass: Harvard University Press, 1910). *Scepticism and Animal Faith* (London: Constable, 1923)

Peter Shaffer, *Amadeus* (London: André Deutsch, 1980, p.119)

Italo Svevo, *Confessions of Zeno* (1923): tr. Beryl de Zoete (Harmondsworth: Penguin Books, 1964, p.58)

Roberto Mangabeira Unger, *Knowledge and Politics* (New York: Free Press, 1975, pp.232 foll.)

W.B. Yeats, *The Resurrection* (1927): *Collected Plays* (London: Macmillan, 1934, p.591); 'The Trembling of the Veil': *Autobiographies* (London: Macmillan, 1955, p.313)

LECTURE TWO

Matthew Arnold, *Culture and Anarchy* (London: Smith, Elder, 1869)

Walter Benjamin: 'Theses on the Philosophy of History': *Illuminations*, tr. Harry Zohn, ed. Hannah Arendt (New York: Schocken Books, 1969, p.256)

John Berger, *Art and Revolution* (New York: Pantheon Books, 1969, p.152)

Denis Donoghue, *Ferocious Alphabets* (Boston: Little, Brown. London: Faber and Faber, 1981)

James Guetti, *Word-Music.* (New Brunswick: Rutgers University Press, 1980, pp.45, 50)

Richard Hoggart, 'Long Arm Tactics': *The Times Higher Education Supplement*, 4 June, 1982

Frank Kermode, *The Genesis of Secrecy* (Cambridge, Mass: Harvard University Press, 1979)

Hilary Mills, *Mailer: A Biography* (New York: Empire Books/Harper and Row, 1983)

Richard Poirier, 'Watching the Evening News': *Raritan*, II, 2, Fall 1982, p.6
John Crowe Ransom, 'Freud and Literature': *Saturday Review of Literature*, 4 October, 1924
Leo Steinberg, *Other Criteria* (New York: Oxford University Press, 1972, p.5)
Adrian Stokes, *Three Essays on the Painting of Our Time* (London: Tavistock, 1961, pp.7–9)

LECTURE THREE

W.H. Auden, 'September 1, 1939': *New Republic*, 18 October, 1939
Roland Barthes, 'The Grain of the Voice': *Image-Music-Text*, ed. and tr. Stephen Heath (London: Fontana, 1977, pp.183–185)
Jacob Brackman, *The Put-On: Modern Fooling and Modern Mistrust* (Chicago: Henry Regnery, 1971, p.60)
John Cage, *M: Writings 62–72*, p.110
Stanley Cavell, *Must We Mean What We Say?* (1969): (Cambridge: Cambridge University Press, 1976, p.202)
Gilles Deleuze, *Francis Bacon: Logique de la sensation* (Paris: Éditions de la différence, 1981)
Jacques Derrida, *La Vérité en peinture* (Paris: Flammarion, 1978). *Éperons* (1978), tr. Barbara Harlow (Chicago: University of Chicago Press, 1979); *Glas* (Paris: Éditions Galilée, 1974). *L'Écriture et la différence* (1967): *Writing and Difference*, tr. Alan Bass (Chicago: University of Chicago Press, 1978, p.279)
T.S. Eliot, 'Marie Lloyd': *The Dial*, December 1922: reprinted in *Selected Essays* (London: Faber and Faber, 1951, p.458). 'Religion and Literature' (1935): *Selected Essays*, p.388
Michel Foucault, *Les Mots et les choses* (Paris: Gallimard, 1966)
Hans-Georg Gadamar, *Truth and Method*, tr. edited by Garrett Barden and John Cumming (London: Shead and Ward, 1975)
Geoffrey Hartman, *The Fate of Reading* (Chicago: University of Chicago Press, 1975, pp.103–104)
Martin Heidegger, 'The Origin of the Work of Art': *Poetry, Language, Thought*, ed. and tr. Albert Hofstadter (New York: Harper and Row, 1971, pp.32 foll)

Frank Kermode, *The Classic* (London: Faber and Faber, 1975, p.134)
F.R. Leavis, *The Great Tradition* (London: Chatto and Windus, 1948, p.11)
Julia Kristeva, *Polylogue* (Paris: Seuil, 1977)
Alastair MacIntyre, *After Virtue* (London: Duckworth, 1981, p.48)
Herbert Marcuse, *The Aesthetic Dimension* (Boston: Beacon Press, 1978, p.6)
Czeslaw Milosz, *The Captive Mind*, tr. Jane Zielonko (London: Sidgwick and Jackson, 1953, p.31)
Nietzsche, *Beyond Good and Evil* (1886), tr. R.J. Hollingdale (Harmondsworth: Penguin Books, 1973). *The Will to Power* (1884–1888), tr. Walter Kaufmann and R.J. Hollingdale (New York: Vintage, 1967). *Thus Spoke Zarathustra* (1883), tr. R.J. Hollingdale (New York: Vintage, 1961). *The Birth of Tragedy* (1872), tr. Francis Golffing (New York: Doubleday, 1956). *The Gay Science* (1882), tr. Walter Kaufmann (New York: Random House, 1974)
Meyer Schapiro, 'La nature morte comme objet personnel': *Macula*, 3: reprinted in J.B. Rhine (ed.), *The Reach of Mind: Essays in Memory of Kurt Goldstein* (New York: Springer, 1968)
Schiller, *On the Aesthetic Education of Man* (1795), tr. Elizabeth M. Wilkinson and L.A. Willoughby (Oxford: Clarendon Press, 1967)
John Searle, '*Las Meninas* and the Paradoxes of Pictorial Representation': *Critical Inquiry*, VI, 3, Spring 1980
Leo Steinberg: '*Las Meninas*': *October*, No.19
Lionel Trilling, 'Dr. Leavis and the Moral Tradition': *A Gathering of Fugitives* (Boston: Beacon Press, 1956, p.104)
David Watkin, *Morality and Architecture* (Oxford: Clarendon Press, 1977)

LECTURE FOUR

T.W. Adorno, 'On the Fetish Character in Music and the Regression of Listening': reprinted in *The Essential Frankfurt School Reader*, ed. Andrew Arato and Eike Gebhardt (New York: Urizen Books, 1978, p.271)
Samuel Beckett, *Proust* (London: John Calder, 1965 reprint, p.64)
John Berger, *Art and Revolution*, p.23
Jorge Luis Borges, *Labyrinths*, ed. Donald A. Yates and James E. Irby (Harmondsworth: Penguin Books, 1970, p.223)

Kenneth Burke, *The Rhetoric of Religion* (Boston: Beacon Press, 1961, pp.14–15)

Stanley Cavell, *Must We Mean What We Say?*, p.207

Nicola Chiaromonte, *The Worm of Consciousness*, ed. Miriam Chiaromonte (New York: Harcourt Brace Jovanovich, 1976, p.239)

S.T. Coleridge, *Biographia Literaria* (London: Dent, 1956 edition, p.12)

Arlene Croce, *Afterimages* (New York: Knopf, 1977, p.338)

E.R. Dodds, *The Greeks and the Irrational* (Berkeley: University of California Press, 1973)

William Empson, *The Structure of Complex Words* (London: Chatto and Windus, 1951, p.434). *Collected Poems*. (London: Chatto and Windus, 1955, pp.46–47)

Michel Foucault, *Language, Counter-memory, Practice*, ed. Donald F. Bouchard (Oxford: Basil Blackwell, 1977)

William Golding, *A Moving Target* (London: Faber and Faber, 1982, p.163)

Julia Kristeva, *Desire in Language*, ed. Leon S. Roudiez (Oxford: Basil Blackwell, 1980, p.138)

Jacques Lacan, *Écrits* (Paris: Seuil, 1966, p.690)

Susanne K. Langer, *Feeling and Form* (London: Routledge and Kegan Paul, 1953, p.113)

Frank Lentriccia, 'Reading Foucault': *Raritan*, II, 1, Summer 1982, p.52

Claude Lévi-Strauss, *Le Cru et le Cuit* (1964): *The Raw and the Cooked*, tr. John and Doreen Weightman (London: Cape, 1969, pp.15 foll.). *Tristes Tropiques* (1955): tr. John and Doreen Weightman (Harmondsworth: Penguin Books, 1976, pp. 67–68)

Charles Morris, *Signs, Language and Behaviour* (New York: Prentice-Hall, 1946)

I.A. Richards, *Principles of Literary Criticism* (1924) (London: Routledge and Kegan Paul, 1960, p.276)

Rainer Maria Rilke, *The Notebooks of Malte Laurids Brigge* (1910): tr. M.D. Herter Norton (New York: Norton, 1949, p.74)

Harold Rosenberg, *The Tradition of the New* (London: Thames and Hudson, 1962)

Ludwig Wittgenstein, *Philosophical Investigations* (1958:1967): tr. G.E.M. Anscombe (Oxford: Basil Blackwell, 3rd edition, 1972, pp.7, 18)

LECTURE FIVE

T.W. Adorno, *Philosophie der neuen Musik* (1949): *Philosophy of Modern Music*, tr. Anne G. Mitchell and Wesley V. Bloomster (New York: Seabury Press, 1973)
Walter Benjamin, *Reflections*, pp.320, 321
Maurice Blanchot, *The Gaze of Orpheus*, tr. Lydia Davis (Barrytown, New York: Station Hill Press, 1981)
David Cairns, 'How to Enjoy New Music': *The Sunday Times*, 16 May, 1982
T.S.Eliot, 'Note sur Mallarmé et Poe', tr. Ramon Fernandez, *Nouvelle Revue Française*, 1 November, 1926
Michel Foucault, 'Revolutionary Action': in *Language, Counter-memory, Practice*, pp.218–233
Paul Griffiths, *Peter Maxwell Davies* (Universe, 1982)
Robert Klein, *Form and Meaning* (New York: Viking, 1979)
Richard Kostelanetz (ed.), *John Cage.* (New York: RK Editions, 1970, p.13)
Leonard B. Meyer, 'Grammatical Simplicity and Relational Richness – The Trio of Mozart's G minor Symphony' : *Critical Inquiry*, II, 4, Summer 1976, pp.693–761
Philip Rieff, 'Fellow Teachers', *Salmagundi*, Summer-Fall 1972, p.27
Harold Rosenberg, *The De-definition of Art*, p.12
Matyas Seiber, 'Schoenberg's Third String Quartet': *Music Survey*, IV, 3, June 1952
Susan Sontag, *Against Interpretation.* (New York: Dell, 1981 reprint, pp.3–13)
Wallace Stevens, 'Notes toward a Supreme Fiction': *Collected Poems* (London: Faber and Faber, 1955, pp.396–397)
Lionel Trilling, 'Mind in the Modern World' (1973): *The Last Decade* (New York: Harcourt Brace Jovanovich, 1979)
Marina Vaizey, 'Art Language': *The State of the Language*, ed. Leonard Michaels and Christopher Ricks (Berkeley: University of California Press, 1980)
Paul Valéry, *Eupalinos, ou l'Architecture* (1921): *Dialogues*, tr. William McCausland Stewart (London: Routledge and Kegan Paul, 1957)

LECTURE SIX

Roland Barthes, *Critique et Vérité*. (Paris: Seuil, 1966, p.79). *Mythologies* (Paris: Seuil, 1957): *Mythologies*, tr. Annette Lavers. (Frogmore: Paladin, 1973, p.151)

R.P. Blackmur, 'A Burden for Critics': *The Lion and the Honeycomb*, p.200

Kenneth Burke, 'Prologue in Heaven': *The Rhetoric of Religion*, pp.273–316

A.C. Charity, 'T.S. Eliot: The Dantean Recognitions': in A.D. Moody (ed.) *The Waste Land in Different Voices*. (London: Edward Arnold, 1974, p.154)

T.S. Eliot, *Collected Poems* 1909–1962 (London: Faber and Faber, 1963, p.219). *The Use of Poetry and the Use of Criticism*, pp.118–119, 148.

William Empson, *Seven Types of Ambiguity* (London: Chatto and Windus, 3rd edition 1953, p.79)

Northrop Frye, *The Great Code: The Bible and Literature* (New York: Harcourt Brace Jovanovich, 1982, p.21)

René Girard, *Mensonge romantique et vérité romanesque* (1961): *Deceit, Desire and the Novel*, tr. Yvonne Freccero. (Baltimore: The Johns Hopkins University Press, 1966, pp.2–4)

Henry James, *The Future of the Novel*, ed. Leon Edel (New York: Vintage, 1956, p.126)

Hans Jonas, *The Phenomenon of Life: Towards a Philosophical Biology* (New York: Harper and Row, 1966, p.261)

Kant, *Critique of Judgment*, Part I, 6: *Selections*, ed. T.M. Green (New York: Scribner's, 1929, pp. 382–383)

Thomas Mann, *Doctor Faustus* (1947), tr. H.T. Lowe-Porter (Harmondsworth: Penguin Books, 1968, p. 89)

Marianne Moore, 'Poetry': *Collected Poems* (New York: Macmillan, 1951)

Flannery O'Connor, *Mystery and Manners*, ed. Sally and Robert Fitzgerald (London: Faber and Faber, 1972)

Paul Valéry, 'Aesthetics': *Aesthetics*, tr. Ralph Mänheim (London: Routledge and Kegan Paul, 1964, p.46)

Philip Wheelwright, *The Burning Fountain* (Bloomington: Indiana University Press, 1968, p.34)

William Carlos Williams, *Selected Essays* (New York: Random House, 1954, p.106)

Ludwig Wittgenstein, *Tractatus Logico-Philosophicus* (1921), tr. D.F. Pears and B.F. McGuinness (London: Routledge and Kegan Paul, 1961, p.150)